"Ready, Always Ready"

The Story of the 148th Pennsylvania Volunteer Infantry

David Kohler

MERRIAM PRESS

HOOSICK FALLS, NEW YORK

2017

First published in 2017 by the Merriam Press

First Edition

ISBN 9781576386255
Library of Congress Control Number: 2017940298
Merriam Press #MH5-P

This work was designed, produced, and published in
the United States of America by the

Merriam Press
133 Elm Street Suite 3R
Bennington VT 05201

E-mail: ray@merriam-press.com
Web site: merriam-press.com

The Merriam Press publishes new manuscripts on historical subjects, especially military history and with an emphasis on World War II, as well as reprinting previously published works, including reports, documents, manuals, articles and other materials on historical topics.

Dedication

This book is dedicated to my three wonderful grandchildren.

Madeleine
Sophia
Wyatt

Acknowledgments

THERE are many people to whom I am indebted who made this book possible. Not the least of whom is my wife, Rogene. She spent many hours listening to passages and making suggestions throughout the entire process of writing this book. Her suggestions and helpful criticisms have been invaluable.

My brother, George, and my sisters, Diana and Lois, were also quite helpful to me. They provided me with their insights and were available for me to discuss various aspects of the book whenever I called on them. My brother, who has assumed the role of custodian of the family genealogical material, supplied me with a photograph of Simeon Bathurst, our great-great grandfather, the narrator of this book.

My cousin, Tom Gouldy, was kind enough to supply me with copies of letters written by our great-great grandfather Jacob Kohler who was a captain in the Pennsylvania Militia and was present at Gettysburg shortly after the battle. Ann Reese, my great aunt, spent an afternoon with us when we were in Pennsylvania doing research and provided many insights. Also, the kind people at the Dean Wetzler Funeral Home in Milesburg, Pennsylvania were kind enough to spend some time with us while we were researching.

We received much help from the personnel at the various battlefield sites, including Gettysburg, Chancellorsville, Spotsylvania and the Wilderness. Last but not least I would like to thank my many friends and acquaintances who have been supportive of me as I trudged along this happy road. They are numerous, and for fear of inadvertently excluding one or more, they shall remain anonymous.

Contents

Introduction

THIS is the story of the 148th Pennsylvania Volunteer Infantry in the Civil War. It is not a history of the Civil War and it seeks only to tell the story of one regiment that was part of the Army of the Potomac from the time it was raised in the summer of 1862, until the end of the war. Most of the specific content about the regiment and its various personnel can be found in a book that is called *The Story of Our Regiment, the History of the 148th Pennsylvania Volunteers.* It was published at the beginning of the twentieth century. Although it has a great wealth of information about the regiment and the Civil War in general, it is not organized as a narrative. Generally, each of the various chapters is a separate story dealing with some specific aspect of the regiment's activity or a specific unit, (i.e. the musician's story, the story of Company A, etc.) and is the work of many members of the regiment.

That book is fairly lengthy and not one you can read through easily because it is not a narrative. Rather, it is a compilation of many separate stories written by many different people with a myriad of different experiences, many of whom expressed differing opinions and viewpoints on the various aspects of the war and what happened at the time. One of the main tasks in putting together an interesting and readable story was to sift through all the stories set forth in that book, choose stories that give an accurate picture of the regiment, and convey them in a way that is both interesting and informative.

Another task faced by an author is to become familiar with all the places that are mentioned in telling the story. This includes not only the battlefields but the routes that the regiment traversed as they proceeded to and from their encampments as well as to and from the battles. It also included becoming familiar with all the towns which gave up their sons and fathers who marched off to war. Fulfilling these tasks provided a depth and understanding that would not otherwise be available to me.

Another thing that is very important for an author, is to be sure he has a thorough grasp of the events that make up the history of the war. This is not an easy task given the multitudes of books written on every possible aspect of the Civil War by a multitude of different people, many of whom had vastly different opinions which they expressed in vastly different manners. It is perhaps impossible to be completely objective because of all the viewpoints and opinions that have been expressed over the years. One way to accomplish this is to go to sources that are as close to the events as possible. One great source is a series called *Battles and Leaders of the Civil War*. This is a series of 32 volumes that was published in the 1880s and contains many articles written by those persons who participated in the war, some of which are unique to this set of volumes. However, it is important to keep in mind that many of these primary sources are the products of the generals who directed the actions, and their accounts may be less than perfectly objective. As a matter of fact, there are several instances in which the editors changed or modified the content of the various accounts. It is therefore important to consider subsequent works that may give more accurate accounts as the result of more intensive and objective study of the events.

Another source that I was fortunate enough to have access to, is a group of letters written by my father's great-grandfather. They were written from Gettysburg shortly after the close of the battle. He was an officer of the Pennsylvania militia and was charged with cleaning up the battlefield and guarding Confederate prisoners of war.

This book is a narrative and not a scholarly work and has, therefore, not been footnoted. I have prepared a bibliography, however, which cites the sources I have directly relied upon as well as books and articles that I have used to gain background information. All direct quotes are marked as such and have been identified in the text.

Since this book is intended to be a narrative, the question arises as to how to do the narration. I have entrusted this task to the spirit of my great-great grandfather, Simeon Bathurst. He was a real person and he was there from the beginning to the very end. Quotes and comments attributed to him in this book are not set apart with quotation marks. They reflect what I believe he would have, or could have said at the time. Quite often they directly reflect the stories and comments made by members of his Regiment as set forth in *The Story of Our Regiment* and I believe them to be an accurate depiction of what happened as witnessed by the participants.

For Simeon Bathurst this was not his first enlistment. When the war began he enlisted in what is known as the ninety day service on April 20, 1861 and served until July 21, 1861 when he was discharged. At the time it was thought that this would be a short war. However that did not happen, and when the call went out for volunteers in the summer of 1862 he reenlisted at Milesburg, Pennsylvania as a private in what was to become the 148th. Pennsylvania Volunteers, was promoted to Corporal, eventually to Sergeant and served until the end of the war. When the war was over he returned to Milesburg where he married and raised a family. For Simeon, the Civil War became a life-long interest and he owned many writings related to the war including the above mentioned history of his regiment and the series *Battles and Leaders of the Civil War*. He treasured the penny whistle and the rifle he took with him when he marched off to war, as well as the badges which he pinned to his uniform identifying him as a member of Company F, First Division, 148th, and Second Corps.

Simeon Bathurst lived a long time. When he left this life at age ninety-eight he took with him many memories that no other person will know. What he did leave to us was a proud heritage and some artifacts that can help us today as we try to understand the great conflict that strove to tear our country asunder; including the aforementioned rifle he carried when he marched off to war, his penny whistle, the badges he had pinned to his uniform, and several books and other volumes published shortly after that great conflict. This narrative reflects not only the things that he experienced, but also many events that he came to be very familiar with through his knowledge of the writings mentioned above.

As previously mentioned, he lived to be ninety-eight years old, and was perhaps the oldest surviving Civil War veteran in central Pennsylvania when he passed away. A newspaper article published in the *Centre Country Democrat* on the event of his ninety-fourth birthday states that he was injured twice, once at Chancellorsville and once at Gettysburg. We know of his lifelong interest in this great conflict because there were many accounts of him making presentations about the war throughout his life.

Of course there is no way that a person today can have direct knowledge of what Simeon Bathurst said. As stated earlier, in constructing this narration I have been very careful to include only information that he would have, or at least could have, experienced firsthand or could have learned from the source material that was available to him. Much of that source material belonged to Simeon, and it has been handed down to me. He gave it to my mother in 1938 two months before he died and she entrusted it to me. The personal artifacts which I possess were entrusted to me by his daughter, my great-grandmother, in about 1964.

Any comments which Simeon makes, through me, in this book that are not directly derived from source material reflect my best efforts to convey how he felt and what he would have said. They have been formulated with the benefit of having some knowledge of the comments and ideas expressed by his daughter, granddaughter and his great-granddaughter (who was my mother).

When I play a tune on his penny whistle, when I hold his badges in my hand or when I examine the books that once belonged to him, I can say "This is the penny whistle he played, these are the badges he had pinned to his uniform when he marched into battle more than one hundred and fifty years ago, and these are the books my great-great-grandfather treasured."

Colonel James A. Beaver, 148th Pennsylvania Volunteers, wounded in action at the Battle of Chancellorsville.

James A. Beaver, Governor of Pennsylvania, 1887-1891. Wounded four times during the Civil War, James Beaver became an active campaigner for Republican candidates, but refused to run for himself, even when offered the opportunity to be James Garfield's vice presidential running mate in 1880. Had he run, Beaver would have become president of the United States when Garfield was assassinated in 1881. In 1886, Beaver became the fourth Civil War general to be elected governor of Pennsylvania.

October 27, 1864: Armed with Spencer repeating rifles, men of Company K, 148th Pennsylvania Volunteers, advance in skirmish line and capture a fort garrisoned by the 46th Virginia Infantry during the Siege of Petersburg, Virginia.

Sergeant Simeon Bathurst, Company F,
148th Pennsylvania Volunteers (circa 1934).

Centre County court house in Bellfonte, Pennsylvania.

Remains of the house at Chancellorsville.

Site of the Boalsburg Academy located in Boalsburg, Centre County, Pennsylvania.

Gettysburg: 148th Pennsylvania Volunteer Monument.

Gettysburg: 148th's position at the start of the wheat field battle.

Chapter 1

Our Regiment is Born

THIS is the story of my regiment, the 148th Pennsylvania Volunteer Infantry. My name is Simeon Bathurst. I enlisted as a private at Milesburg, Pennsylvania and served until we were mustered out at the end of the war. The 148th Pennsylvania Volunteers was actually my second unit. Like many young men, I enlisted as soon as the war broke out, on April twentieth, 1861. This was what was called the "ninety day service." At that time we thought it would be a short war. I was in Company F of the 4th Pennsylvania Volunteers and was discharged on July twenty-first. 1861. Later, while a member of the 148th, I was promoted to the rank of Sergeant and was mustered out at the end of the war.

Much of what is in this story I witnessed first-hand. Some of the events and stories have come down to me from my comrades in arms. Other information comes from newspaper articles published at the time the events occurred. Of course this was before the great invention of the telephone, but the telegraph was in common use. As a result there were many stories published in the newspapers shortly after the events took place, and they were widely circulated. Still other information comes from a volume that is the history of my regiment, referred to in the introduction of this book, as well as other books about that great conflict, which I acquired, and over which my great-great grandson has gained custodianship over the years. He has used those resources to reconstruct my story as I would have told it if I were still here.

Let me tell you how the book *"The Story of Our Regiment"* came into being. As was often the case, members of our regiment had reunions after the war. Some of the veterans of the regiment decided that it was important and necessary for our friends, families and any other people who might be interested in that great conflict known as the Civil War, and of the part we played in it, to know what really happened. Some of us felt that there should be an accurate picture of that time to let people as yet unborn know about the war that sought to render our country asunder. We wanted our grandchildren to know what we did, how we lived, what happened in camp and on the march, how we fought and how our blood soaked into the ground of Virginia and Pennsylvania.

We therefore decided to put down on paper stories which we told each other, and to share the reminiscences we had about all aspects of our Regiment from its formation until the close of the war when we were finally able to return to our families; having successfully fought to preserve our great Union. Included in that book, which was published about 1900, were the stories from our leaders as well as the stories of our various companies and of the many specialized units and personnel that made up our Regiment. This includes such groups as the musicians, the quartermasters, the surgeons, etc. Since that book came into being at the very beginning of the twentieth century, it has become a valuable resource for many people.

Let me begin. The dark clouds of war had settled over the towns and villages of Centre County nestled among the valleys of the Allegany Mountains in central Pennsylvania where I lived. In November of 1860 Abraham Lincoln had been elected President of the United States, receiving 180 of a possible 303 electoral votes and forty percent of the popular vote. He had declared that "Government cannot endure permanently half slave, half free..."

Reaction in the southern states came swiftly. By the end of December South Carolina had seceded from the Union, followed in close succession by Mississippi, Florida, Alabama, Georgia, Louisiana, and Texas. In February the Confederate States of America had been formed with Jefferson Davis, a West Point graduate as President.

The beginning of hostilities followed closely on April 12, when the Confederates opened fire on Fort Sumpter at Charleston, South Carolina. On April 15, four years to the day before President Lincoln would die, having been struck down by an assassin's bullet, he issued a Proclamation calling upon 75,000 militiamen for three months service. It was obvious from this call that Union officials thought the war would be a short affair. The bombing of Fort Sumpter, however, started a bloody conflict that would rend the country, causing untold misery, setting brother against brother, and father against son for four long years.

From the very beginning and up until the present day many of those people who fought for the Confederacy and who believed in their cause blamed the Union side for the war and stated that it was really the fault of the Union states. They claimed, and some still do, that they were forced into a war merely to defend their property rights; in other words to defend their right to own slaves, among other things.

A year passed and it had become obvious that this was not going to be a short war. On June 28, 1862 the President put out a call for 300,000 troops and a few days later, on July 1, a call for an additional 300,000. All throughout the United States citizens answered their country's call. The men of Centre County responded, and thus was born the 148th Pennsylvania Volunteer Infantry.

The two calls for men in such rapid succession brought a rash of activity to Centre County and the rest of Pennsylvania. In their haste to get a regiment quickly organized, the volunteers who had enlisted in their various companies of citizen soldiers from Centre County, descended on Camp Curtain at Harrisburg with fewer companies that then constituted a regiment. Although it was referred to as a Centre County regiment, as it turned out, only seven of the ten companies were actually from Centre. One company originated in each of the following counties: Jefferson, Clarion and Indiana. My company, Company F, was one of those companies from Centre County that had members who were residents of nearby counties.

Hand bills had been published and distributed throughout the county calling for a public meeting to be held at the county court house in Bellefonte. The courthouse at Bellefonte is an impressive structure with a colonnaded front that looks out upon the square. It had been damaged by a fire in 1855 but had since been restored. It is situated between Howard and High Streets looking down towards the creek and the spring which gives the town its name; "beautiful fountain" in French.

It was a Saturday, August the second, and a meeting was held to promote the enlistment of men, as well as to propose the means to pay an enlistment bounty of fifty dollars for each volunteer. For most of the men, volunteering was a matter of honor and was considered a patriotic duty. The citizens also knew that if they did not meet their quota there would be a draft and it was the consensus of those present that a draft should be avoided at all costs.

A motion to float bonds in the amount of ten thousand dollars would be necessary to pay the enlistment bounty. The motion passed without dissent and the county swung into action. The next step was to find the right men to raise the required companies. This was an important step, and as the community leaders were well aware, this would be an important factor in determining the makeup and effectiveness of the various companies which would make up the regiment.

Not only would these chosen leaders recruit the men for their companies, they generally would become the commanding officer of that company.

The United States had a very small standing army so the overwhelming number of combatants, both enlisted men and officers, were to come from the ranks of these volunteer regiments. In Centre County, as throughout the Union, the person who organized the company generally became its captain. The captain was usually elected by the members of his company, however those elections were quite often mere formalities.

Commissions to recruit were issued by the Adjutant General of Pennsylvania.. Those people who were commissioned to recruit would soon be at work within their own localities, conducting their recruiting with the assistance of such leading citizens as the local judge Hon. James T. Hale, attorneys H. N. McAllister, John G. Kurtz and Capt. William H. Blair. The various companies were recruited throughout August, generally with great success.

Initially all areas of the county were well represented with one exception. Those were the townships which had largely Pennsylvania Dutch populations. The very southern part of Centre County was settled rather early in the history of the county by folks of German descent. When the road known as the Buffalo and Penns Valley Turnpike opened in 1810, passing through the southern part of the county, it allowed the Pennsylvania Dutch from the eastern part of Pennsylvania to easily migrate to this part of the country. They settled three towns; Aaronsburg, Rebersburg and Millheim. Some of my Dutch friends told me that Millheim is German for "The home of mills." That was a real good name for the town. The Elk Creek runs through there and it is a natural location for all the mills that sprung up along the creek. As long as I can remember there's been both a sawmill and a gristmill there. These people, the Pennsylvania Dutch folks, had landed in America from Germany and settled in southeastern Pennsylvania considerably earlier than the more recent German immigrants who populated our cities such as Philadelphia and Pittsburg. Their primary language was still German, however. Unlike their more newly arrived countrymen and their Anglo-Saxon neighbors who were strongly Republican, they were more likely to lean towards the Democratic Party rather than the party of Lincoln and were less likely to back the Union cause. This made the recruiting of them much more of a job.

One of those towns, Aaronsburg, was founded at the end of the 18th century by a Jewish merchant named Aaron Levy. He laid out the town in a grid pattern, hoping that it would be named the county seat. Another thing that he did was to present the new residents of the town with the Silver Communion set as a token of his goodwill. Today Aaronsburg is a little town about a mile east of Millheim and although Aaron Levy's efforts to have his town become the county seat were unsuccessful, his ecumenical act of kindness has been remembered to this day.

A delegation of our leading citizens, the same ones who spoke at Bellefonte, tried to persuade their German neighbors to become volunteers. Remember, that in 1862 traveling from the county seat at Bellefonte was a day's journey through a very hilly area on largely unpaved roads without the luxury of automobiles, and it was no small task. They went to the towns of Rebersburg, Millheim and Aaronsburg, hoping to help them see the light. Not only did they try to impress the residents of their duty to serve, but they pointed out that those communities who failed to reach their quotas would be subject to the draft in proportion to their failure to volunteer. One of those Pennsylvania Dutch residents who was highly respected in the community replied to their visitors from Bellefonte that if they were going to face the draft, they would merely fade away into the mountains where they could not be found till after the war. They probably could've done that. The area was heavily forested as it still is today.

There is a possible reason why the German residents of our county were not as eager as they might be to volunteer. In America there was a large group of people who were referred to as "nativists." They were also called "know nothings." This was group of English speaking people who had been living in the United States for a while and considered themselves to be better than newly arrived people, especially the Germans who spoke some "strange" foreign language. As a matter of fact there were many cities in this country that actively discriminated against their German-speaking residents. In the state of Massachusetts Germans were not allowed to vote until after they had been citizens for two years. This, as well as many other forms of discrimination, is something that certainly would have caused ill will among the German citizenry.

Indeed, many of the German-speaking residents in our country came here because they were discriminated against. Many of the Pennsylvania-Dutch residents had been severely discriminated against in their own homelands, and came to America because of religious persecution in their former countries. I think you can understand an attitude when people might say "Why should I fight for this country if they don't treat me as an equal?"

The recruiters, however, apparently had satisfactory answers for our German cousins. They told them that the war was likely to last for a long time and if they stole away, or "skulked" as we called it, they would be forced to live off the land in hiding for a long time. After convincing the Germans that they were not trying to act on behalf of themselves but to assist their German neighbors in making a correct decision, they saw the light and agreed that two German companies could be raised, one by R.F. Forster and one by Andrew Musser. To my knowledge there was no mention of any ill feeling that might have existed among the Germans in our county, although they lived separately from the English speakers. The multiethnic makeup of our regiment would make it special. We would not be just American, but German also. Those two companies made us one of the Union's genuine German-American regiments. There were many totally German and Irish regiments but we represented a true cross-section of our country. As a matter of fact, my own company started out with an Irish captain. More about that later.

The efforts at recruitment in the so-called German townships having borne fruit, on the twenty-fifth of August, a group of one hundred recruits, mostly farm boys, standing in irregular rows assembled in front of the hotel in the town of Rebersburg. There they took the following oath that initiated them into the great force that would do battle throughout the remaining years of the war, bringing both glory and death.

"You and each of you acknowledge that you have voluntarily enlisted as a soldier in the Army of the United States of America, for the period of three years, or during the War; and each of you will serve them honestly and faithfully against all enemies whomsoever, and that you will obey the orders of the President of the United States and the orders of the officers appointed over you, according to the Rules and Articles of War, and this as you shall answer to God on the Great Day"

Today a monument stands at the site to commemorate that event. It is engraved with the names of those brave young men who volunteered to go off and support their adopted land. There were many tears in the eyes of the assembled crowd that day as they watched their young men, some barely out of childhood, as they began the transition from civilian to military life. Many mothers and fathers, brothers and sisters, friends and relatives wept, some silently, at the thought that their precious young men could be bidding them farewell for the very last time. The new citizen soldiers seemed less affected, perhaps looking forward to the great adventure that lay ahead.

After swearing them in Lieutenant Fetterman addressed the young recruits directly with instructions and a warning. " You are now soldiers in the United States; you will meet at this place on the twenty-seventh of this month to be taken to the front, and if you fail to report, you will be arrested as deserters." This admonition by their swearing in officer gave the first inkling to many of the young recruits that this was not a game; it was deadly serious business. To be arrested and charged with desertion could mean execution.

After two days in which the new soldiers prepared themselves for whatever was in store, they left their homes in and around Rebersburg in various farmers' rigs and set out for Lewistown, arriving that evening, after a trip of thirty miles. The next day it was off to Harrisburg and Camp Curtain by train. Supper that first evening in camp was their first disappointment—— cold pork, bread and coffee! Little did they know that this was goodbye to the bountiful home cooking they had known their whole lives. Goodbye to apple butter and jellies. Goodbye to homemade pies and cakes, noodles and dumplings, succulent roasts. Hello cold pork, hard tack and coffee!

During the month of August scenes similar to this were repeated throughout the county. The pleasant village of Boalsburg was home to one of our well known schools, called the Boalsburg Academy. Summer vacation had ended and the young men and women had returned to their beloved school to start another year. The school was all abuzz. The students gathered near the hall knew that something important was happening. What was it? Was there a Union victory of some sort? Or maybe some sort of setback?

In response to a young girl's question, somebody blurted out "President Lincoln has called for more volunteers and Professor Patterson is going." At that moment their beloved principal appeared and all eyes turned to him. At the ripe old age of twenty-five he was not much older than some of his students. He addressed them in a slow and dignified manner. "Yes, I am going and not alone, for I shall take as many of my brave boys as can and will go with me."

According to Sophie Keller Hall who was there that day along with her older brother, the lessons learned were not Latin, Mathematics or History. They were lessons of courage, hope, love of home and country. Professor Patterson spoke of his obligations as a citizen and an able bodied man to protect his country in its time of peril. He felt that his time to serve had come if he were to be true to his country and himself. He also made a heartfelt appeal to those students who were able to follow his example and march off to defend their country.

Later on, the solemn tolling of the bell at the "Old Stone Church" called the citizens of Boalsburg to a meeting. Distraught mothers, sisters and sweethearts sang, or rather tried to sing, a patriotic song through their tears. The imposing figure of Judge McAllister from Bellefonte spoke in a way that convinced all present of their sacred obligation and duty. At the conclusion of McAllister's speech Professor Patterson rose and stood before the assembled congregation. In his hand he held the school roster. He told those assembled of his decision to enlist in the service of his country. He then made an announcement. "Today I shall read the roll of my students for the last time. Those who are willing and able to serve with me. answer by saying "Ready." He then proceeded to go down the role in alphabetical order to a chorus of "Ready" as the young men signified their willingness to follow their master. Sophie waited with dread for the name she hoped she would not hear. "Keller"—"Ready!" Thus was born another company of the new regiment.

On August thirteenth the new company numbering one hundred and twenty-seven men gathered in Boalsburg. After an emotional farewell they set out first for Potters Mills having been joined by the balance of enrollees. An election of officers was held. Robert A. McFarlane who had been commissioned to recruit the company was named its Captain, and as could be expected Professor Patterson was elected First Lieutenant.

After dinner was served by the people of the community, the new company traveled over the mountains to Lewistown. From there they proceeded to Harrisburg by train, arriving at 1:30 A.M. In the morning they marched out to Camp Curtain and on the eighteenth of August they were sworn into the United States service. On September 8, 1862 the regiment was organized and the company from Boalsburg became officially Company G of the 148th Pennsylvania Volunteer Infantry.

The little town of Boalsburg distinguished itself two years later when citizens of the town placed flowers on the graves of veterans. Thus they laid claim to being the first place in the country to have a Memorial Day, a tradition that developed into our national holiday, celebrated at the end of May each year.

The other companies which became members of the regiment all had similar experiences. The details were different but the effect was the same. All of the new companies enlisted in or around their home towns, elected officers, proceeded to Camp Curtain and would be organized into the 148th Pennsylvania Volunteers. The next chapter of their military history would soon begin.

Chapter 2

My Company

MY company was one of the seven who were considered Centre County companies, but its makeup was a little different from the others. This was because ours was raised a little differently from those other companies.

As stated earlier, when the call went out to raise a regiment, men would be commissioned to raise a company. Often these were men who had previous military experience or men who were otherwise prominent in their community. They were generally leaders in the community with skills that enabled them to recruit, organize and then lead a group of men. Also, they were quite often from the same close knit community. This fact is reflected in the many so called "ethnic regiments" that comprised perhaps fifteen percent of our Union forces. They were generally German or Irish regiments. Their leaders had usually been military or political figures in their home countries. After their arrival at our shores they became the leaders in their new communities. They had come to the United States to escape political repression or because they had been on the losing side in the German Revolutions of 1848 or some other repressive action in their home countries. We will learn much more about these so-called German regiments when we talk about the battle of Chancellorsville.

We got to know some of the Irish soldiers really well because the 148th was camped next to the Irish Brigade much of the time. We learned that these so-called ethnic regiments had been raised in areas where there was a high population of Irish or German folks, and they were raised by men from their own areas, many of whom had extensive military service in their native lands. For instance, there were several German regiments from Cincinnati, Ohio, reflecting the great number of Germans living in and around that city.

Boggs Township, in the middle of Centre County, was not very heavily populated. Our little town of Milesburg was located there the Bald Eagle and Spring Creeks came together. It was founded before the turn of the nineteenth century by Colonel Samuel Miles who established an ironworks there in 1795. Miles was a veteran of both the

French and Indian and the Revolutionary Wars and is buried in our little Cemetery at Milesburg.

Centre County had many iron furnaces because of the abundant iron ore which could be found in the area. An ironworks at Milesburg was built to convert the rough product from these furnaces into iron that could be used commercially and shipped more easily.

Martin Dolan was an Irish tavern keeper in Milesburg and he kept a tavern at a place called Central City near the Milesburg train station. His tavern was a brick building near the point where the Bald Eagle and Spring Creeks come together. The building survives, but not as a tavern. It is now the location of the local funeral home.

Although he had no military experience whatever and was not what anyone would call a civic leader, Martin Dolan possessed an easy way of talking to folks because of his chosen profession, Further, he had a delightful Irish brogue. These were his main qualifications for raising a company and becoming its leader. It must be said that his qualifications worked much better for being a tavern keeper than an army officer.

In spite of his obvious lack of qualifications, Martin Dolan answered his country's call and decided to raise a company for the Centre County regiment. Besides, if he raised a company, he could be commissioned as an officer, and "Captain Doyle" sounded very good to him.

I was one of his regular patrons, lifted many a glass at his establishment and was there when he put out the call at his tavern for people to enlist. I answered the call and thus began my second stint in the military.

At about this same time there was a log rolling at the farm of a certain Perry John Lucas in Snow Shoe Township northwest of Milesburg. A log rolling was a community event where all the neighbors gathered to help clear the land, roll the logs into heaps and to prepare the land for planting. It was a time of hard work as well as community fellowship. Snowshoe was about fourteen or fifteen miles away and it was up a fairly steep grade from Milesburg to the town of Snowshoe. Nevertheless, who should appear but the jovial Martin Dolan. Because of the distance and the steep grade, it would've taken him the better part of a day to travel from his tavern up the mountain to his destination.

Snowshoe was an important place at that time because it had a mine which provided soft coal for the ironworks down in Milesburg, and a railroad had been constructed several years earlier to transport the coal down to the ironworks. The trip would've been much easier if he had been able to travel there via the railroad. We don't know what type of conveyance he used, however.

Once there, he announced the call of President Lincoln for men to join the Union cause. With his impressive Irish brogue and genial manner he also announced his intent to recruit a company, as well as the date and time those interested should rendezvous at his tavern in Milesburg. At the appointed hour several of the log rolling recruits from Snow Shoe made the trip down to Milesburg in order to become members in Martin Dolan's fledgling company. In spite of this, the company was still short of its full complement

Fortunately, other men brought squads to help fill out the company. Included were William Wilson who brought a squad from Potters Mills, James Duncan from Spring Mills and George Steffey from Stone Valley in Huntington County. Among the recruits was a youngster from Snow Shoe of only sixteen named William Lucas. He had also served as I had previously, in what was known as the "three months service." This was a good thing for our company because he was the only one of us (myself not included) who had any military training whatsoever. He became the "de facto" First Sergeant since nobody else in our ragged assemblage had the faintest idea about anything military. This included our erstwhile captain who did not seem to have any interest in or aptitude for military leadership. Young Lucas was really our leader at that time.

We did manage to arrive at Camp Curtain on the twenty-ninth of August. When we finally arrived there, and the regiment was ready to be officially organized, we were still short of a full complement of men for a company. This problem was solved by assigning men who did not already have a company to us. Martin Dolan assumed the role of Captain in our company. It should also be noted that he was self-appointed..

There is a telling comment in the story of our regiment about our "erstwhile commander" that showed he had no military experience whatsoever and very little aptitude for command. It is said he was glad to leave his squad, upon its arrival at Harrisburg in the hands of Lucas, who marched it into Camp Curtain, secured tents and other camp requisites and provisions and established the squad in comfortable quarters. However, an unpleasant thing happened to William Lucas shortly after we arrived. A stranger showed up, unannounced, and let it be known that he had been appointed First Sergeant of our company. Young Lucas did not complain but assumed his position in the ranks with the rest of us. I must add, however, that through his diligence and skill he eventually rose to the rank of Lieutenant.

Camp Curtain was a place where the soldiers assembled when the call to arms brought thousands of newly made soldiers to serve the Union cause. It had been the grounds of the Dauphin County Agricultural Society on the northern outskirts of Harrisburg. Those in charge had wanted to call it Camp Union but many of the local Pennsylvania residents insisted in calling it Camp Curtain, in honor of our governor. Governor Curtain was a Centre County boy and he had attended the Bellefonte Academy. We were proud of our Centre County Governor, and the men of our new regiment also wanted a Centre County Colonel to lead them, as well.

One task remained for our fledgling regiment. We needed a leader. The Captains of our companies knew whom they wanted for their Colonel and they set out to have him appointed. Lt. Colonel James A. Beaver was a native son and, for the citizens of Centre County, he was their man; so they wrote a letter to Governor Curtain asking for him to be promoted to Colonel and assigned as the commander of their regiment.

Their plan hit a snag. Lt. Colonel Beaver was already attached to the 45th Pennsylvania Volunteers. Governor Curtain replied that he could not discharge an officer in active service to serve in an as yet unorganized regiment.

There proved to be more than one way for our regiment to skin the cat! Beaver had been informed of the situation and wrote a letter to H. N. McAllister at Bellefonte. He suggested that if all the captains signed a letter stating that their regiment was ready to be organized, and they wanted him to serve as their Colonel, he would try to obtain his own discharge from the 45th in order to assume leadership of the new regiment.

The letter was written and sent with an attached endorsement from the governor that read "This request is made with my approbation, and for the reasons set forth. I unite in the petition. [signed] A. G. Curtain, Governor Pennsylvania." Fortunately for us, the request was granted by Secretary of War Stanton.

In the meantime the seven companies from Centre County had arrived in Camp Curtain at Harrisburg, in conveyances provided by the citizens of the county, and by train. The last was my own, led, at least nominally, by Martin Dolan, leaving from Milesburg on the 29th of August. On the fourth of September Beaver received his discharge and arrived at Harrisburg on the 6th. The regiment was officially organized with the addition one of company each from Clarion, Jefferson and Indiana counties. It was equipped on the eighth.

We were a brand new regiment, and had not trained or been battle tested. Nevertheless, the 148th Pennsylvania Volunteers had gone to war.

Chapter 3

Off to War

A FTER securing his discharge Colonel Beaver set out for Washington to settle his accounts from the 45th Pennsylvania Volunteers, his former regiment, and sent his horses overland by his colored servant, Ike. On the way up to assume command of our regiment he took time to visit his brother who was a lieutenant in the 51st Pennsylvania. Little did he know that it was a final farewell. His brother was killed fewer than two weeks later in a gallant but useless charge across the stone bridge at Antietam. Since our Colonel arrived at Camp Curtain on the sixth of September, it took a couple of days for us to get the companies fully organized and outfitted

Let me add a word about our equipment. Along with the basic necessities of the infantryman we were issued the old Vincennes rifles, and they weren't worth a damn. First of all, the rifling was very shallow and that severely affected their accuracy. They were absolutely worthless at over two hundred yards. Second, they were .69 caliber and the caliber for the standard Springfield rifles was .59. That meant we might not be able to get the right ammunition when it came time for a fight. Third, they were equipped with the old fashioned and very cumbersome saber type bayonets.

We left for Cockeysville, Maryland by train on the ninth of September to guard the railroad. This job was important because, as you know, Maryland was a border state and it was known that some of Maryland's southern sympathizers had threatened to burn the railroad bridges and tear up the railroad. This would have caused havoc for the movement of Union troops to the important sites in Virginia.

We were lucky. It was at the bloody battle of Antietam near Sharpsburg, Maryland that took the life of our Colonel's brother. It was a terrible defeat; the most deadly battle in our country's history. We could have been sent there, but we were a totally green regiment and unprepared for combat. It was either through an act of Providence or the decision of some wise general that sent us to guard the railroad rather than directly to the front where we would have served mostly as cannon fodder. I am absolutely certain that this wise act saved many a life of the fledgling soldiers of the 148th Pennsylvania Volunteers.

Our regiment was spread out for several miles guarding the railroad and it was hard to get all the companies gathered at a central location. We finally assembled in one place at the very end of September for our first general inspection. You cannot imagine the unpleasant surprise that was in store for both us and our colonel.

The nicest thing you could say about us was that we were green troops. Just days before most of us had been young farmer boys, students at the academy or tradesmen. Some of us were there merely because we had been regulars at Martin Dolan's tavern. We were a sorry sight!

We had no idea that our Colonel was a stickler for clean and orderly uniforms, polished brass buttons and spotless white gloves. Not only that, precise and orderly drill was maybe even more important to him. For Col. Beaver, cleanliness and orderliness was next to godliness, and godliness won battles. That first inspection revealed to both the colonel and us the monstrously huge task that lay ahead. The colonel must have thought "Why did I leave the 45th for this motley bunch of ragamuffins?"

He went up and down the ranks, unbuttoned our coats to expose dirty shirts, tore apart our knapsacks to expose the soiled garments hidden under a top layer of clean shirts, upbraided us for the poor condition of our weapons and generally condemned our slovenly manner. We truly hated this man who was our colonel. It didn't matter that he was from Centre County. After our longest day in the army so far, we cursed him. For his part there was not much he could do or say except to stand back and slowly shake his head in disappointment and disgust.

This routine continued on a regular basis. At first we thought of him more as a strict tyrant than as an able commander. We were subjected to regular formal as well as informal inspections of our camp, the quarters and outposts. We were also learning the drills and maneuvers that were so necessary for infantry units. As time passed we were learning to respect our colonel and I suspect that the respect was mutual. We were starting to learn that the colonel really did have our best interest at heart and we also were starting to understand that what we learned now would be very important later. The time we spent guarding the railroad in Maryland was very important for our whole regiment. It was a time for us to learn the skills required to be a soldier. Without this intense period of training, who knows what would have happened to us when we were introduced to combat.

"Ready, Always Ready"

Company members themselves soon came to realize that they were not exactly the most professional and competent company in the regiment. One of the members wrote in our regimental history:

"The boys of F Company were rather enterprising and soon became acquainted in the neighborhood, frequenting a little village two or three miles below Cockeysville, known as Texas, consisting of a Tavern and a group of houses in the neighborhood of the celebrated lime quarries of that region. The company soon learned that however its captain might be deficient in military knowledge and ability to enforce military discipline, the colonel was not only never tired but seemed to be ubiquitous and the impression generally prevailed that he knew every man in the Regiment, could call him by name and knew more of his dailies habits than some of them cared to have known. It is possible that in this they might have been mistaken but, from the colonel's knowledge of what every man in the company did and of those who visited Texas and other places in the neighborhood, as communicated to the captain in rather vigorous style, there was good ground for believing that little went on in the Regiment which was not in some way brought to the attention of its commanding officer."

We did not realize it at the time, but this was sort of a basic training for us, and we were very lucky because many green troops were sent directly into battle and the results were quite often disastrous for them. We grew to understand how important this time was for us later on as we witnessed the results of inadequately trained soldiers being sent to the front and slaughtered by the Confederates at Cold Harbor.

Also, we were starting to observe some things that helped us understand him as a real person and someone who had our best interests at heart. One thing, though, he hated profanity; and you know how soldiers can swear. He was always trying to hold down that practice by issuing orders and giving personal reprimands to the offenders. One day after witnessing a particularly colorful outburst he said "Do you realize that under the Articles of War you could be fined for the profanity you have uttered in my hearing?" The offender reached into his pocket and promptly tendered a dollar to the colonel. Colonel Beaver really didn't want to take the man's money, so he fumbled around in his pocket and said "I'm sorry I don't have any change." The man promptly replied "Never mind the change, Colonel. I expect I'll swear it out."

We lost our first man less than two weeks after arriving in Maryland to guard the railroad. One of the men from Company G drowned in the Gunpowder River. During the next month, October, we lost four more of our comrades. They all died in the hospital. One was from my company. The Colonel told us that it was from improper care of themselves in the matter of diet and exposure. I don't know. They just got sick and died. A study of the records will show you that just about as many men died from sickness and accidents as died in battle.

During that early time in the Army we spent many hours in battalion drill, learning how to march and do all the necessary maneuvers that are important to an infantry regiment. Those long hours spent in drill would stand us in good stead once we got into combat.

By our monthly inspection at the end of November we had shown great improvement and we were starting to look and act like real soldiers. That is, *most of us* were starting to look and act like real soldiers. One company was very disorderly and not prepared. This incident was chronicled in the story of our regiment but the offending company was never mentioned by name. That is probably for the best, because we eventually became a proud regiment with each and every company performing as it should.

The colonel suspected that some of the officers were behind this mini rebellion, and he was probably correct. Right then and there he had those officers arrested and the company marched off the field. I don't know what kind of punishment was meted out to the officers but I do know that there were no more disorderly inspections of the 148th. Under the sure and steady hand of Colonel Beaver we were being molded into a fit and proper regiment, one of which we could all be proud.

Chapter 4

Our First Winter Quarters

AFTER three months of guarding the railroad and learning the basic skills of a soldier we got our marching orders. On December the eighth all of us who were able went to Baltimore by rail. About eighty of our men were too ill to travel. They were sent to hospitals at York and other places. Unfortunately many of them died. Most of those who recovered joined us later. As you can tell from reading this, not all the casualties of war happened on the battlefield. Many of our brave boys were struck down by illnesses or accidents. As I mentioned earlier, figures compiled since the war show that the number of men who perished because of illness was about the same as those who were killed in combat.

When we got to Baltimore the regiment had to march through town in order to arrive at the Baltimore & Ohio tracks. The B&O was the only railroad to run from Baltimore to Washington and they had no connection with the line that we had been guarding, the North Central. Some of our boys were a little bit nervous because we had heard stories about the bad reception some of our troops had received from confederate sympathizers as they passed through the city. That was not the case with us. The people we encountered as we marched along all seemed friendly enough. We were fed at the Union Relief Headquarters, boarded the train and were off to our nation's capital.

After we arrived at Washington we received our orders to proceed to Falmouth, Virginia, which would be our winter camp. We started out on the eleventh of December. All the steamers were in use carrying stores and equipment to the Army of the Potomac so we were forced to set out on foot. This proved to be a fortunate happenstance for our regiment. Had we traveled by steamer, we would have arrived in time for the unfortunate Battle of Fredericksburg, another one of the Union's costly defeats.

It was a disaster for the Union forces. Not only did we suffer a crushing defeat, our forces bombarded the city of Fredericksburg causing much damage to the town. After we took the town our forces proceeded to loot and destroy property with impunity. These acts created a long-standing hatred for the Union forces by the citizens of Fredericksburg and surrounding area. Also, that disastrous battle cost General Burnside his job as commander of the Army of the Potomac. It was a good thing for us we were not there.

Our route from Washington was to march out along the Potomac on the Maryland side and cross over to Virginia from Liverpool Point to Acquia Creek. The first night out was particularly unpleasant because it rained. There was frost and the roads were muddy. Going was slow and we didn't reach Liverpool Point until the fifteenth. Those were four very unpleasant days.

Many of us were really excited at seeing such a wide expanse of water for the very first time. Most of us had never been around a body of water bigger than the Bald Eagle or Spring Creek, except maybe for the Susquehanna. Our feelings of excitement quickly changed to foreboding when we saw the wounded soldiers being taken from the steamers which would carry us across this wide expanse of water into enemy territory. They were victims transported from our bloody defeat at Fredericksburg. It was the first time we had really gazed upon the face of war, and the face of war was an ugly one, but one with which we would become all too familiar.

Our regiment boarded the steamers during a steady rain and stayed on board at Acquia Creek till we were a bit dried out. From there we proceeded on foot to our camp site at Falmouth, Virginia. It was a place just north of Fredericksburg, about ten miles into Virginia.

For those of you who have never been to that area, the distances were not that great, at least on the map. Our train ride from Baltimore to Washington was only about forty miles, and the march down to Liverpool Point from Washington was about forty-five miles as close as I can reckon. However, when you have to march forty-five miles with a pack on your back, carrying a rifle on muddy roads in the rain; forty-five miles can be a long way. That march from Washington to Liverpool Point taught us an important and somewhat unpleasant fact. We learned that when we weren't soaking the ground with our blood, it was with sweat.

When we reached the place where we would build our camp, we received our assignment within the Union forces at Falmouth, Virginia. We became members of the First Brigade, First Division, Second Army Corps, Right Grand Division, Army of the Potomac. The 148th Pennsylvania Volunteer Infantry had found its home.

It was at about this same time that the famous poet Walt Whitman arrived at Falmouth. He had been informed that his youngest brother, George Washington Whitman, had been wounded at Fredericksburg and he wasted no time coming to find his brother. Luckily for him, his brother had not been seriously wounded. That slight wound to Whitman's brother had a profound effect on the care of many injured warriors.

The great poet witnessed the horrors and pain of war so vividly that he spent the rest of the war in Washington caring for the wounded and working to improve their care. At age 43, he was already a well-known poet although his works were not universally accepted or admired. Many thought them downright immoral and he also was not universally accepted or admired as a good person either. Many of the nurses at the hospitals found him to be an unpleasant person and thought he loved the wounded patients a little *too* well. Nonetheless he spent countless hours visiting and comforting the wounded soldiers in the hospitals in and around Washington.

He held a strong belief that the military leaders and politicians (some of whom belonged to both groups) could not tell the real story of the war. Out of this belief sprang his collection *Drum-taps* which let people know about war as he saw it, rather than just heroic stories of marvelous victories. Here is one of the poems from that collection that illustrates his deep feelings about the war:

"Dirge for Two Veterans"

The last sunbeam
Lightly falls from the finish'd Sabbath,
On the pavement here – and there beyond, it is looking,
Down a new-made double grave.

Lo! The moon ascending!
Up from the east, the silvery round moon,
Beautiful over the house tops, ghastly phantom moon;
Immense and silent moon.

I see a sad procession,
And I hear the sound of coming full-key'd bugles,
All the channels of the city streets they're flooding,
As with voices and with tears.

I hear the great drums pounding,
And the small drums steady whirring;
And every blow of the great convulsive drums,

Strikes me through and through.

For the son is brought with the father;
In the foremost ranks of the fierce assault they fell;
Two veterans, son and father, dropt together,
And a double grave awaits them.

Now nearer blow the bugles,
And the drums strike more convulsive,
And the day-light o'er the pavement quite has faded,
And the strong dead-march enwraps me.

In the eastern sky up-buoying,
The sorrowful vast phantom moves illumn'd;
('Tis some mother's large, transparent face'
In heaven brighter growing.)

O strong dead-march you please me!
O moon immense, with your silvery face you soothe me!
O my soldiers twain! O my veterans, passing to burial!
What have I also give you.

The moon gives you light,
And the bugles and the drums give you music;
And my heart, O my soldiers, my veterans,
My heart gives you love.

No general could have written those words.

Chapter 5

Setting Up Camp

HAVING arrived at our appointed location, we soon discovered that this would actually be a pretty good place to build our winter quarters. The front of our regimental line was longer than most and we claimed the land covered by our front as part of the regiment's territory. This gave us plenty of space to lay out streets and build quarters for the regiment. We laid out the streets parallel to a public road which would prove to be advantageous for receiving our supplies and equipment.

We arrived ahead of our supplies and so it was necessary to bivouac until our tents arrived. For those who don't know military terms, "to bivouac" means we were forced to camp out in the open. We had only the blankets and ground cloths that we carried in our packs for shelter. From the time we left Acquia Creek until our tents finally arrived after several days, it was cold and rainy, so we were left shivering and drenched. We were forced to improvise as best we could to stay warm and dry in December's wet and cold. It was a happy day when the wagons finally arrived with our tents.

There were plenty of pine trees in our camp area that we used for constructing our winter quarters. My company, Company F, had two of the best woodsmen in the army. They were much older than most of us but they could do about anything possible with an axe. Their names were Wash Watson and Bill Perry. Watson had a long white beard and looked to be about sixty. Perry was clean shaven but seemed to be about the same age. Together they were the foundation of our pioneer corps. They could fell the trees, dress the logs, construct the various buildings that were required, split logs for corduroy roads or do anything else that was required of them.

With their skills we could construct huts of logs and use our tents for the roofs. Wash Watson became more or less a guardian angel for Colonel Beaver. He did everything he could to make the colonel's life a little easier and more comfortable, whether it was fixing his tent fly while we were on the march or building a comfortable hut with matched and dressed logs for our winter quarters.

We did not realize it initially but our position on the extreme right flank of our brigade was very advantageous. Positioned next to us was the famous Irish Brigade commanded by General Meagher, a proud native of Waterford, Ireland. These were fierce fighters but their ranks had been severely depleted by the recent disastrous battle of Fredericksburg. They were composed mainly of the 63rd, 69th and 88th New York Infantry. After Antietam they were joined by the 28th Massachusetts Infantry, and as their name implies they were mostly made up of Irish soldiers.

Their antics and high spirit provided us with great entertainment. There is a saying that was popular among the boys of our regiment. "The Irish know how to do three things really well; sing, drink whisky and fight." We often had arguments about which of those three things they did best. There were times when I was lucky enough to join them with the penny whistle that I had brought with me from Milesburg.

Another thing the Irish Brigade did was to supplement our boring and sometimes meager diet. I don't know why, but they always seemed to have more and better food than boys of the 148th. Our Irish brothers did, however, share some of their extra foodstuffs with us sometimes—not willingly, and sometimes not knowingly.

They had an abundance of good flour, more than they could possibly use. At least that's what some of our boys thought. They hatched a sure fire plan, and soon a whole barrel of flour came up missing from the Irish commissary. Of course it was missed! Not only were the Irish infuriated, but so was our colonel.. He had some reason to know who the guilty parties were, based on some of their previous antics, and maybe from some inside information.

He went directly to their hut, and standing on one of the bunks announced that the criminal behavior of stealing rations from the other units must stop, and that those found guilty would be severely punished. No flour was ever found though, and nobody was ever severely punished as a result of the mysteriously disappearing flour.

If the Colonel had only known! He had been standing on the missing flour. Literally, standing on the flour. The thieves had dug a hole big enough to hide the barrel of flour, put the barrel in the hole and moved a bunk directly over the purloined flour. When the colonel delivered his stern warning he had been standing on that very bunk! Needless to say, we had an abundance of hotcakes for quite some time.

Also, we knew that the Irish had more than enough molasses to go around. We had none! The problem was that a barrel of molasses was much too heavy to be spirited away, besides, by now the Irish were on to us and had placed guards in front of their commissary tent.

Not to be outsmarted, our Centre County boys arrived at an ingenious solution. Two of our boys went over to the commissary tent and engaged the guards in polite conversation. With their attention diverted, one of our boys armed with a fairly wide board snuck into the tent from under one of the far walls. He plunged the board straight into the barrel of molasses and gathered up a goodly amount. One of our comrades lifted up the back sidewall of the tent to allow our boy to exit the tent. He ran back to his hut turning the board as he went. This kept the molasses from dripping off as he ran. Once back in the hut, willing hands scraped the board into a waiting kettle. We now had molasses for our hotcakes!

Some people would call these acts of thievery. Not so! We were all in the same army. We all deserved to eat as well as possible, so some of our boys tried to bring that about. There are those who might say that, like Robin Hood, we were robbing the rich to feed the poor. Today you might call it a redistribution of wealth.

As the winter of 1862/63 closed in upon us, the regiment was slowly being transformed into a proper fighting unit. Unbeknownst to us, the Colonel had been campaigning for new rifles from the very beginning. As far back as October, Colonel Beaver had sent in a report about the poor quality of our weapons and had requested more serviceable rifles. Shortly after we arrived here the Colonel called for an inspection, the object of which was to show the unserviceability of our Vincennes rifles and have them condemned as unfit for service. By the way, I was one of the lucky ones. There were not enough rifles to equip the entire regiment so I took my trusty old gun. This was a great advantage for me. It was my Ross rifle, very light weight and easy to carry on a long march. It would have been great at picking off rebs.

Well, we did have the inspection and the result was that our rifles were condemned as unfit for service. Finally we would be issued our Springfield rifles. Rumor was that Judge Hale from Bellefonte put in many a good word for us which proved helpful in the campaign to get our new weapons. The new rifles arrived at the beginning of February and we would be ready when duty called us to battle.

While we trained and further prepared ourselves for spring and the inevitable battles to come, illness and death did not take a vacation. Our Colonel McFarlane took sick and was escorted home by Dr. Potter of Bellefonte who was a surgeon in the 145th Pennsylvania. Col. McFarlane had contracted typhoid fever, returned before he was fully recovered and was forced to leave the service because of his ill health. We lost many men that winter because of typhoid and other diseases. Life was not easy for the soldiers living this new way, being exposed to the rigors of an army camp in winter.

For some it was just too much, so they chose what they thought was an easier way. For them it was to be a quiet and stealthy trip home, away from the cold and the rigors of army life. For many of those would-be freedom seekers the result was total disaster, and the loss of much more than their freedom. They were caught and branded as deserters. These unfortunate wretches suffered the ultimate punishment.

It happened not long after St. Patrick's Day. Everybody was in good spirits because we had witnessed the high jinx and celebrations of our brothers next door, the Irish Brigade. Our mood was immediately transformed, however, from light-hearted to somber. The whole division was drawn up in two lines facing each other. To our far right a procession had started. There was a mighty sound like thunder as all the drummers in the whole division roared into action. Above the din of the drums you could hear the somber strains of "The Dead March" played by the fifes. Soon you could see three obviously distressed men slowly marching along, each being closely followed by a soldier with his bayonet clad rifle at the ready. As the procession approached we could see that the buttons and insignia had been ripped from their uniform coats.

At first that's all we noticed about them. Then as one turned his head toward us we could see that it had been shaved on one side. The left side of his head looked normal but the right side was bald. As they passed we could see a placard fastened to the back of each uniform coat. In bold block letters it proclaimed "COWARD." When the unhappy procession had reached the end of the line, the booming drums ceased their symbolic cannonade and the three forlorn men stood alone. They were given one command. "About Face." With downcast eyes they faced their executioners. The command was given and three Union soldiers whose only wish was to get home safe and sound left this life forever.

Unfortunately, executions for desertion were not uncommon. Something that has always seemed a contradiction to me is that the condemned were given spiritual counseling prior to being shot to death. Chaplains were assigned the unhappy task of administering counseling and giving comfort to these unfortunate men as they faced their demise. Whatever happened to "Go away my son and sin no more," and more importantly "Thou shalt not kill?" William Henry Stevens was a chaplain and gave this account:

I performed the most solemn duty on the second that ever crossed my pathway. I was sent for on Wednesday night to visit a young man at the division headquarters, condemned to be shot for desertion. When I went to see him the General asked me to become his spiritual advisor and to officiate at his execution. I could not refuse as there was no Chaplain in the Regiment to which he belonged and the young man desired a Methodist Chaplain, and I was one of the only two in the Division. I found him very ignorant of all religious subjects and seeing that I would have to be his teacher as well as spiritual advisor, I commenced at the alphabet of religion. He readily comprehended the plan of redemption and on Thursday night was converted. I have no doubt of his genuine conversion. He was too ignorant to be susceptible of deception or hypocrisy. He sang hymns until the Provost Marshal came in and told me that they were ready. He arose, put on his cap, took my arm and marched behind his coffin, borne by four men, half a mile, approached his grave, took his cap off, heard his sentence read. I then prayed and bade him goodbye. The Provost Marshal then blindfolded him, he then seated himself on his coffin and in a moment was pierced by eight balls, six in the body and two through the head. All of which time he never moved a muscle—was as composed and cheerful as I have ever been in all my life. He made this remark when on the way to the place of execution, when I exhorted him to continue to trust in Christ, "Chaplain it seems to me that the Lord goes with me wherever I go." He belonged to the 66th New York. Name, Adam Small, aged twenty years, has a mother and four brothers. Strange to tell, though a few weeks ago I stood off and saw the execution of two men, I was so shocked that I could hardly stand on my feet, I led this young man to the place of execution, attended him in his last moments and saw him shot, put in his coffin and buried without the least emotion or unpleasant feeling.

Eighteen days later he wrote another letter home relating the same duties.

"We marched from Bull Run on Monday, arrived here on Tuesday, lay in the woods yesterday, were ordered into regular camp this morning, worked hard all day fixing up nice and held prayer meeting in the evening, came to my quarters and found orders to march at seven-thirty in the morning. I have no idea where we are going, hence I write. On last Friday I led a second young man out to his grave, seated him on his coffin and saw him shot. These are duties which require courage."

Through the month of April we continued to sharpen our skills. We were reviewed both by the President and Governor Curtain, much to the satisfaction of both. Also during that time we lost several officers, both to discharge and to resignation. As a result there were quite a few promotions within the ranks. I was promoted to the rank of Corporal on the seventh of April and served in that capacity until February 1865 when I finally became a sergeant. The day before I received my corporal's stripes we were finally paid. As a result of this happy event our chaplain was granted a leave of absence so he could deliver the money we did not need for personal expenses to our families back in Centre County. This was a duty he never failed to perform in an honest and faithful manner.

One of the duties we were given, and learned to dread, during our winter encampment was picket duty. For those who have not heard that term, the pickets act as guards, sentinels and lookouts for the army. This is an extremely important job because if there were no pickets or if they were not performing their duties properly, the enemy could sneak up upon us and cause a great defeat.

When men are selected for picket duty they are under orders of an officer who is known as the "officer of the guard." He stations the pickets out ahead of the lines in such positions as are well concealed from the enemy, but where they can hopefully observe any enemy movement. The pickets must also be placed in such a position that they can easily come together and act as a first line of defense should the need arise. They must also have a clear path to quickly get to camp if the need to warn the camp becomes necessary.

The pickets are supplied with a sign and a counter-sign. Today you might call it a password. If a picket encounters somebody, they give the sign and if the other person cannot give the counter-sign they are to detain the person and if the person starts to flee they have orders to shoot the intruder.

You can see that the safety of the entire army is dependent on these men who have been chosen to protect and guard the camp. Sleeping on duty is a crime of the highest order for a picket. If found asleep at his post, the picket is subject to being shot. All soldiers must learn from the very beginning that being chosen for picket duty is not something to be taken lightly and that the consequences for failure to perform properly are the most severe.

Chapter 6

Off to the Battle of Chancellorsville

SPRING was upon us, and with it the life and death struggles that had become the lot of the Army of the Potomac would soon be rekindled. On the twenty-seventh of April we received our marching orders. The next day the regiment formed and marched up the Rappahannock for about five miles, and four miles the following day. Both days we were hindered by rain which slowed our progress. On Thursday the thirtieth we crossed the Rappahannock, and marched till about 11:00 P.M. Little did we know that this would be the beginning of the battle of Chancellorsville. For the Union forces it was to be the second bloodiest of the war.

I can only give a first-hand account of the battle from the viewpoint of a corporal in the 148th. Much of the battle's account, as it appears in this book, comes from sources other than what I myself witnessed. I am sure you would understand if you could see the wide expanse and the many thousands of people who were present and participated in the battle. The front stretched for many miles. Some of the description comes from newspaper accounts, some from my comrades in arms and much from the written accounts of those who made the plans and attempted to carry them out.

The plan as I understand it was for the Fifth, Eleventh and Twelfth Corps to cross the Rappahannock upstream of the rebel forces and attack them from the west. As you remember, our regiment was part of the Second Corps. Two divisions from our corps were to sneak across and join the Fifth Corps in pushing the rebs away from the river. This was to be our role. We took with us eight days' worth of rations when we left our camp at Falmouth so we would have sufficient for both the march to our crossing point and several days of battle without the need to resupply.

The other part of the plan was to have the First and Sixth Corps under General Sedgwick cross the Rappahannock below Fredericksburg and attack from the east. They called this a double envelopment. The idea was to catch Lee's forces in the middle. Also one division of our corps and the Third Corps would remain in camp at Falmouth, across the river from Fredericksburg, to act as a diversion and draw attention away from our movements.

I was not a person who was trained as a writer, but there were people in our regiment who were, and could tell the story much better than I. One of those people was Henry Mayer of company A. He was from Rebersburg which is one of the German towns in the south part of our county and his native language was German, but he had an excellent command of the English language and was a skillful writer. After the war he spent time as a teacher, a superintendent of schools, state representative, and a justice of the peace. This is how he described going into battle and he tells the story much better than I.

"Going into battle is a serious matter, an ordeal which the bravest dread. Outwardly, some may not exhibit a sign of fear, but it requires all the willpower of the brave man is able to put forth to stand in the ranks to be shot at---one feels as though he were suspended over eternity by a single thread. ... With their names and places of residence legibly written on the fly leaf of diary or bible, or stamped on metallic badges securely fastened to their clothes, for the purpose of identification in the event of being left dead, upon the field, steadily our rather sad looking boys moved in the direction of the firing in front. Notwithstanding the seriousness of the occasion, we could not refrain from smiling at the sight of myriads of cards strewn all along the whole breadth of the road, and among the bushes along the sides, lying thick as autumnal leaves. The troops that passed along the road before us to enter the battle flung away their decks of cards for the reason that none of the boys would have a report go home, in case they should be badly wounded or killed, that there was found on their person, a deck of cards.

Other scenes productive of graver thoughts now presented themselves. Streams of wounded soldiers were coming back from the battle then in progress; wounds of all descriptions met the view; some of the men dragged themselves along by the aid of rude crutches; some came with a shattered arm dangling by their side and others more seriously hurt in an ambulance or stretcher."

On Friday morning, the first of May we had advanced to what the officers thought was a beautiful position along the Orange Turnpike. It was about a mile and a half in front of Chancellorsville looking toward Fredericksburg. It must be remembered that the hamlet of Chancellorsville was little more than a single building situated at the crossroads of the Orange Turnpike and the Orange Plank Road. On orders from general Couch, we had marched by file into a commanding position to the left of the road. We performed this maneuver with great skill in spite of the fact that we were a new regiment and had never been in battle, much to the surprise of General Couch. Through an aide to General Hooker, that order was countermanded and we were ordered to take up a new position to the rear. That order infuriated our leader, Colonel Beaver, who had put his heart and soul into transforming his new charges into a battle ready regiment. We had no choice, however, so we assumed our position in reserve.

I should add at this point that I received my first wound at the battle of Chancellorsville. I was wounded in the right leg but not severely enough to disable me. Given the state of medical care at the time and the extreme conditions under which we fought, I consider myself to be a very lucky man. Many of those who fought at Chancellorsville and were wounded, perished in the subsequent fires that had resulted when the woods were set ablaze. Also, severe wounds often resulted in amputation of the limb. We all saw the mountains of arms and legs outside of the temporary hospitals, the result of the surgeons performing their grizzly but necessary handiwork.

After all the maneuvering of the last two days, the battle actually started at about noon on Friday the first of May when our forces met the 12th Virginia along the Orange Turnpike and pushed them back towards the Confederate line. Three brigades under General Sykes pushed forward along the Orange Turnpike while our foe, General Jackson, affectionately known by his men as "Stonewall" moved his troops forward astride Sykes right flank. In the meantime our General Williams was moving his Union troops forward along the Orange Plank Road, south of the Turnpike to be met by Anderson's Confederates. The Confederates on Sykes right under General Rodes drove the Union forces back.

Under pressure on both Sykes flanks, Hooker who had succeeded Burnside after Fredericksburg, ordered Sykes forces back. At this time we had been advancing along the Orange turnpike and were in the rear. Sykes forces passed through our formations as they were pursued by the rebel forces led by Jackson. The day's action ended in the evening. Jackson's forces had, in the meantime, now again proceeded forward and outflanked us on the right. My company along with others from our regiment had been placed on picket duty and was away from much of the action so we did not actually witness the goings on and as a result we suffered many fewer casualties than the rest of our regiment.

Sedgwick's forces had crossed the Rappahannock to face the Confederate forces from the east as part of the double envelopment, but Lee had divided his army foiling Hooker's plan. There were rebel forces facing Sedgwick in the east, but the bulk of his forces advanced in a westerly direction towards Chancellorsville.

Nobody knows for sure why Hooker with his overwhelming advantage in numbers chose to withdraw and assume a defensive position, but many people felt that this move early on is what really cost us the battle. On the second of May our forces had dug in near Chancellorsville and were awaiting the enemy. Unbeknownst to our forces, Jackson had managed to work his way around our right flank by way of the lesser used roads. Lee had taken the unprecedented step of dividing his forces again and sent the majority of his troops with Jackson on his successful secret flanking movement.

General Sigel had been in command of the Eleventh Corps, on the far right, but he had resigned because of serious disagreements and what he viewed as slights. The Eleventh Corps was made up largely of German units who were very loyal to their former leader. Documents and information that has come to light since the war would confirm that the Eleventh Corps had been treated unfairly. There had been rampant discrimination against the Corps because of its largely German makeup. General Sigel wrongly assumed that he would be reappointed to his old position, but his assumption was incorrect and it resulted in very dire consequences to the Corps as well as to the entire Army of the Potomac.

The German soldiers of that corps loved and respected their German leader whom they viewed as one of their own. He was replaced by the one armed General, O.O. Howard, a conservative New Englander, who exhibited little, if any, understanding of the cultural differences between the largely German forces which he now commanded and the traditional Anglo-Saxon forces which made up the majority of the Union army.

Hooker had warned General Howard who commanded the Eleventh Corps about possible Confederate movement on the right and was assured that the Eleventh Corps was prepared. In the afternoon Jackson's forces struck the right flank and utterly surprised Howard's troops. Many people claim the Eleventh Corps broke and ran. Whether that is true I cannot say but I do know that they retreated in some disorder. I also know that our colonel attempted to stem the tide of retreating soldiers without great success. Two of the Eleventh Corps divisions were commanded by Generals Steinwher and Schurz, and known as German divisions. English language newspaper articles throughout the country were filled with articles about how the German troops had broken and run. Many of these papers blamed our terrible loss at Chancellorsville on German cowardice.

As I have mentioned earlier, there was much anti-German sentiment in the country that manifested itself with an attitude known as nativism. This attitude was particularly strong in some of our cities where there were high percentages of recent immigrants including those from Germany and Ireland. Consequently, after the battle was lost those with anti-German bias found a convenient scapegoat. There were congressional hearings held to determine the causes of this terrible defeat. Many of those who testified were very quick to place the blame on the German soldiers and their leaders. Those who testified conveniently forgot to mention the bravery and the excellent fighting skills those very same Germans had exhibited at such earlier battles as at Cross Keys and the Second Manassas. The fact that there were many reports of Confederate movements along the right of the Union line and that these reports had been ignored or dismissed by the commanders because they had been made by the "Dutch" troops, who were considered to be unreliable, was never brought to the attention of the Congressional committee. The English-speaking press was unanimous in its condemnation of the Eleventh Corps and condemned its soldiers as cowardly Germans who panicked and ran from the battle as fast as possible.

Those who were present at the battle know that the Eleventh Corps had been surprised by an unexpected attack from the flank by Stonewall Jackson, one of the most skillful generals of the Confederacy. Many of those who were present and actually experienced what happened would probably have testified much differently. It is very doubtful that our generals would admit to the Congress that they had been outmaneuvered and outgeneraled by a superior leader from the opposing side.

Many people have subsequently theorized that this unfair criticism had a long-term positive effect on the Germans. What it did, was to unify the Germans in the United States. We must remember that at this time Germany did not exist as a separate country. It was a collection of separate states which were great rivals of each other. A Bavarian would not consider serving with a Prussian, nor would a Saxon with a Swabian. What this event accomplished in America predated what Bismarck accomplished in Germany by many years.

One of our surgeons from the 148th, Dr. Fisher, who was present at Chancellorsville, wrote his impressions of events that day in *"The Story of Our Regiment"* and his story does not talk about German cowardice as much as it gives a first-hand account of what he witnessed. This portion of his narration commences in the morning, and gives an account of what happened that day from his perspective.

"During the forenoon a rebel battery, or at least a portion of one, suddenly made its appearance on the face of the ridge to our left front, not more than half a mile away. I remember the thrill of terror which came over me, as I looked over the field close by and saw it covered with the mass of boys in blue, fearing the result, if the battery was allowed to open upon them, but my fears were soon allayed. One of our artillery men in the neighborhood cited this piece and fired and, before the enemy's battery could un-limber, the air fairly rang with the cheers from our boys as they saw a caisson explode as the result of the well-aimed shot. A second shot exploded a second caisson and the battery, from which I feared so much, left unceremoniously, without firing a shot. The cries of the wounded and burned rebs could be distinctly heard and I was told that some of our boys ventured over and brought into our line one of the poor fellows who had been terribly burned by the explosion.

A large brick building, known as the Chancellor House, was General Hooker's headquarters. About four o'clock in the afternoon I strolled up in that direction to see what was going on. Inside General Hooker was with a large number of general officers, and their staffs, on the porch facing the woods or heights opposite. An occasional bullet from a sharpshooter in front would strike the house but fortunately no one was hit. One of these bullets struck a brick by the side of Dr. U. Q. Davis, our Chief Surgeon.

About this time I saw a line of battle forming a few hundred yards in front of the house. My brother Frank (General B.F. Fisher) was at that time Chief Signal Officer of the Army of the Potomac, and I was told by him that this line, under the command of General Geary, intended to make a charge into the woods and drive out or capture the rebs who were in our front. Having never seen a charge, I thought I would accompany the line of battle, although it was not in our corps. We went in with a rush and a yell but the Johnnies were ready for us and our lines didn't stay long. We came back quicker than we went in—at least those who were unhurt. About the time the bullets began to fly thick about me, I became forcibly impressed that I was not in my proper place and that, if I were hurt, I would get no sympathy, as

"Ready, Always Ready"

my place was with my own regiment. That thought hastened my steps but my surprise cannot be imagined, when I got out of the woods, to see the whole line of our troops right up with me.

I went again to headquarters and was watching the reforming of General Geary's line, when an Aide rode up to a group of officers about General Slocum and said that General Geary wished permission to have the artillery shell the woods. I heard General Slocum say: "Tell General Geary to please wait a little, we have another object in view."

It was just at this moment that an entirely unexpected occurrence took place and one which changed the entire program. A tremendous yell came from our right front. There was no break in it, but one continual roar. Then there was wild hurrying and confusion amongst our officers. My brother told me that General Jackson had charged in on our right and was driving in the eleventh Corps. The yell was now accompanied by an incessant roar of musketry and soon the artillery joined in it, but, over it all, could be heard the terrible yell of the twenty thousand rebels who were forcing back and endangering the entire right wing of our Army. Everything was at once turned in the direction of meeting this unexpected attack and it was only by the most urgent haste and the use of all the troops at command that the progress of the enemy was stopped and their reaching the road to the river prevented.

Wishing to see and know all about the fighting, I walked down the road toward the place where the struggle was going on and, whilst on my way, saw two captured rebel regiments with their flags still flying. I could not understand it at the time but was told afterwards that they in mistake, marched right into our lines in the woods in column and that our officers, seeing them come, ordered our troops not to fire but to lie down on the ground, until they advanced sufficiently far, so that they were entirely surrounded. Then one of our Colonels rode up to their commanding officer and told them that he had better surrender, as they were entirely within our power. Seeing this to be the case, the officer handed over his sword with the surrender of his command.

I did not go far until I met with such a mass of men coming back that I was carried back with them. When I returned to the Regiment, Col. Beaver came to meet me and inquired what the matter was. I well remember the reply I made to him and also his reply to me. I told him that the rebel General Jackson had charged the eleventh Corps and had completely beaten it and that on the morrow this Army would be completely whipped. I did not stop to consider that I was speaking in the hearing of our men who had never yet been under fire. The colonel immediately straightened himself up and said: "Doctor, this Army whipped. The Army of the Potomac cannot be whipped."

This was not the end of the doctor's narrative, but at no time did he indicate or imply that the Germans fled in terror or that they exhibited any cowardice.

Dr. Fisher was not the only surgeon who wrote an account of the battle at Chancellorsville. Dr. Carl Uterhard was from Rostock in Germany. He came to the United States with the express purpose of serving in the Army. He was assigned to the 116th New York Volunteer Infantry which was composed of about half Germans. They were part of the Ninth Corps. He was present at Chancellorsville and wrote home about the battle [translated].

" [...] I'm afraid the newspaper report about the unfortunate battle at Chancellorsville, in which our Army Corps played a major role, will have filled you with concern about me [8 II.: is unscathed]. It was the first battle I was in, but it was enough. I never, not for even a moment, had any feeling of fear for my own life, despite the heaviest rain of bullets, because such massive slaughtering of one's fellow human beings does not permit any concern for one's own small self to arise. But upon sober reflection, one realizes what madness it is to put one's life in such danger. Those who are shot and die immediately are the lucky ones; those who were wounded and left behind on the battlefield are the most unfortunate men in the world. Hundreds of our men starved on the battlefield, died of thirst—or of madness brought on by the scorching rays of the sun burning straight down on them. Hundreds burned to death in the woods, when the grass and the underbrush, desiccated by the sun, chanced to catch fire. Hundreds died in the teeming and overcrowded hospitals, where we could hardly help those poor souls, we had no bandages, nothing to eat, nothing to drink. During the most strenuous work while hungry and parched left us doctors so weak and faint that we were in despair. We had a hard, hard time of it, and I hope to God I shall never get into such a situation again. I can't understand how I managed as well as I did [11 II.: several days without food and drink]. During the night it poured down with rain, and since I was only wrapped in a blanket, under God's great sky, lying on the ground with my boots for a pillow, I woke up in the morning, soaked from head to toe, with no coffee to quench my thirst, no crust of bread to still my hunger. ... Then all of a sudden we heard a rustle in the woods behind us, we were struck by bullets, and then thousands of men suddenly dashed out of the woods, fleeing wildly, trying to reach the woods on the other side. Finally I caught my

"READY, ALWAYS READY"

breath and managed to get to the other side of the road, where some regiments were still standing in battle formation, trying to stop the men from fleeing and ready to receive the enemy. The generals and officers struck the soldiers with their sabers to get them to stop running, but they just kept on fleeing. I rode back toward the enemy to look for my Regiment, but I couldn't find it, because after having been attacked four times with the Colonel killed and 128 men lost, it had withdrawn from the advancing enemy. I was now about 200 paces away from the enemy, and [...] So I turned around and galloped back to our battery as fast as I could, because I thought I would be safest there for a moment. There were eight cannon there maintaining a steady, terrible barrage of fire aimed at the enemy coming out of the woods and preventing them from making an advance [...] But then we saw large numbers of enemy artillery, rattling out of the woods, and they took up position and directed horrendous fire at our battery. The first shots already killed a large number of artillery men; the battery turned around, broke away, and I went with them as fast as I could toward the woods about 500 paces away. Then the enemy artillery aimed its devastating fire at everyone who was fleeing, and I saw that almost all of the officers who had been riding near me had been shot off their horses. So I jumped off and ran, leading my horse toward the woods on the double. Right in front of the woods I met my chief surgeon and our druggist; finally we got to the road: forty to fifty of the wounded had dragged themselves to a log cabin there, so we stopped together with some other doctors and started to bandage them up. I had finished bandaging three men and was just about to cut a bullet out of the back of a fourth, when suddenly the rebels, close on the heels of our men, stormed toward our house, spreading death with their shots. Our men turned around while they were fleeing and shot back at the rebels who were bearing down on them. We lay down flat on the ground, trying to stay out of the crossfire we were in. Finally the rebels advanced so far that we were no longer in any danger from the shots of our own men but then the rebels stormed at us, although they saw we were doctors, they called out *All right* and pressed on. Every now and then a rebel officer came riding up, and so bit by bit we lost everything we owned—my horse, my bag, my coat which had my revolver in it, everything gone to the devil. Finally the noble enemy colonel came by who gave us some guards, but they couldn't do anything but try to protect our lives, which were to be seriously endangered two more times.... We were prisoners for two weeks and had to survive hard, hard times. From early morning to late at night the most strenuous work taking care of the wounded. All and all we have about 1,500 wounded here. All these men were wounded in the short three or four hour battle of Chancellorsville on the evening of May second, and even more were killed. Seven thousand prisoners and 30 cannon were captured by the enemy. The dead and wounded were lying around as thick as turnips in the field. Those poor fellows—a day and a night of solid rain drove all those who could not be put somewhere inside almost to despair—their bloodcurdling wails filled the air. Those who died were fortunate, and we could not be of much help, because we were in enemy territory and were prisoners, we had nothing, not even the bandages we needed to dress the wounds. We suffered from such hunger and thirst we all thought we would die. Every day we hope to our ambulances would arrive to get us and the wounded, but we always hoped in vain. On the eighth day a wagon from our side finally did arrive, waving a flag of truce for protection, and they brought us flour, crackers, bandages, milk, and liquor. On the 14th day the long-awaited ambulances finally crossed the Rappahannock. On the 15th we packed up our entire hospital into about 130 ambulances and departed from enemy territory.... As for me, I hope I will never again come under fire as a physician, and I will make sure by staying thousands of paces away from the fighting. Now I know all about this swindle I can resign anytime I want to—I signed up for three years of service, but I can leave the Army anytime if I want to resign, like some doctors do every day, because the hardships are all too strenuous. All of my belongings that I lost, including my horse, and my Negro, who is also gone will be paid for....[Brackets in this letter indicate editing made by the original editors and translators.]"

In the years following the battle there has been much information that should put to rest the theory that the Germans acted in a cowardly way during the battle of Chancellorsville. As stated above, the many reports of Confederate movement opposite and to the right of the Eleventh Corps finally came to light. Unfortunately, such pieces of intelligence were disregarded and often passed off as unreliable because they had been provided by the Germans. Also, suggestions that General Howard should perhaps reposition the extreme right of his line to face west were ignored. If the troops would have been repositioned they would have been able to face Jackson's troops and put up an effective defense. As is shown by history the disposition of our troops on the extreme right of our line made it impossible to conduct an effective defense, and Jackson's brilliant flanking attack led to a disastrous defeat for the Union forces. For those not familiar with the way battles were fought, the sides lined up facing each other, and would fire at each other or charge a defensive position on a broad front. If one side could maneuver around to the side of the opposing force they could charge forward with very little opposition because the opposition forces would be in a line perpendicular to the charging force. This would make it impossible for the defenders to fight effectively because their line would not be facing their opponents.

Back to the battle, it was during this day that our colonel was severely wounded. Witnesses have said that he twirled around and fell to the ground, his sword clattering away. He was immediately attended to and carried from the field. At first it was feared that the wound might be mortal, but luckily it was not.

The battle was proceeding and balls were flying thick and fast, but some men from the regiment dragged him away from the action, found stretcher bearers and got him to the hospital. The surgeon, George Potter, had somehow been informed of his being shot and had a table waiting. The doctor made his initial examination and was able to give our colonel some encouraging news. The ball which had struck him had also struck a gutta percha pencil he had been carrying. The pencil was shattered but in deflecting the ball it prevented the ball from entering Colonel Beaver's abdominal cavity. That wound would have surely been fatal. It can truly be said that a pencil saved our colonel's life.

General Jackson who was affectionately known as "Stonewall" by his men would not be so lucky. That night while scouting out the enemy he was shot and wounded by his own men. He lost an arm but initially survived. Several days later he succumbed to his wounds and the Confederate cause lost one of its most loved and one of its greatest generals.

One of Jackson's aides wrote an account of his leader's last battle which was published in a series of thirty-two short volumes titled *Battles and Leaders of the Civil War*. They came out a short twenty years after the war and give an accurate picture of events told by the people who were actually there. The writer of the piece quoted below was Rev. James Power Smith. He was a captain and an assistant adjutant-general in the Confederate forces. This part of his account commences at about eight in the evening.

"...I had reached an open field on the right, a mile west of Chancellorsville, when, in the dusky twilight, I saw horsemen near an old cabin in the field. Turning toward them, I found Rodes and his staff engaged in gathering the broken and scattered troops that had swept the two miles of battlefield. "General Jackson is just ahead on the road, Captain" said Rodes; "tell him I will be here at this cabin if I am wanted." I had not gone a hundred yards before I heard firing, a shot or two, and then a company volley upon the right of the road, and another upon the left.. A few moments farther on I met Captain Murray Taylor, an aide of A.P. Hill's, with these tidings that Jackson and Hill were wounded, and some around them killed, by the fire of their own men. Spurring my horse into a sweeping gallop, I passed the Confederate line of battle, and, some three or four rods in its front, found the general's horse beside a pine sapling on the left, and a rod beyond a little party of men caring for a wounded officer. The story of the sad event is briefly told, and in essentials, very much as it came to me from the lips of the wounded general himself, and in everything confirmed and completed by those who were eye-witnesses and near companions.

When Jackson had reached the point where his line now crossed the turnpike, scarcely a mile west of Chancellorsville, and not half a mile from a line of Federal troops, he had found his front line unfit for the farther and vigorous advance he desired, by reason of the irregular character of the fighting, now right, now left, and because of the dense thickets, through which it was impossible to preserve alignment. Division commanders found it more and more difficult as the twilight deepened to hold their broken brigades in hand. Regretting the necessity of relieving the troops in front, General Jackson had ordered A. P. Hill's division, his third and reserve line, to be placed in front. While this change was being effected, impatient and anxious, the general rode forward on the turnpike, followed by two or three of his staff and a number of couriers and signal sergeants. He passed the swampy depression and began the ascent of the hill toward Chancellorsville, when he came upon a line of Federal infantry lying on their arms. Fired at by one or two muskets (two musket-balls from the enemy whistled over my head as I came to the front), he turned and came back toward his line, upon the side of the road to his left. As he rode near to the Confederate troops, just placed in position and ignorant that he was in the front, the left company began firing to the front, and two of his party fell from their saddles dead, ...Spurring his horse across the road to his right he was met by a second volley from the right company of Pender's North Carolina brigade. Under this volley, when not two rods from the troops, the general received three balls at the same instant....The writer reached his side a minute after, to find General Hill holding the head and shoulders of the wounded chief. Cutting open the coat-sleeve from wrist to shoulder, I found the wound in the upper

"READY, ALWAYS READY"

arm, and with my handkerchief I bound the arm above the wound to stem the flow of blood. "

Captain Smith goes on to tell the harrowing story of how Jackson was carried from the field, received first aid, and of the wounds that resulted in the amputation of his arm late that night. When General Lee was informed of Jackson's misfortune he penned the following note:

"General: I have just received your note, informing me that you were wounded. I cannot express my regret at the occurrence. Could I have directed events, I should have chosen, for the good of the country, to have been disabled in your stead. I congratulate you upon the victory which is due to your skill and energy. Most truly yours R. E. Lee, General"

Gravely wounded, Jackson lingered until the afternoon of the tenth of May when he passed away, as his friends said " over the river, where, in a land where warfare is not known or feared, he rests forever 'under the trees.'"

Chapter 7

The Battle of Chancellorsville Concludes

AFTER our colonel was injured and taken from the field, Major Fairlamb took over command of the regiment. Our second Corps was to the left, several miles away from Jackson's charge and my company, Company F, was on picket duty facing Fredericksburg. Those companies in the line were subjected to a murderous cross fire from Jackson on the right and Lee's forces from the front. As a result, the regiment suffered severely and we lost many good men. Our regiment had been divided. My company's position was very fortunate for us because we were away from the main action and had very few casualties.

Some of the other companies were not so fortunate. D. H. Young was a member of Company D and he wrote a letter to a friend soon after the battle and he related his experiences on May third

"You wish me to give you a full account of myself. Well, the enemy we encountered was lying flat on the ground partly concealed in the brush and leaves at a distance of about twenty-five yards from us in fact the head of our company (D) was only about half that distance, they fired into our ranks before we knew they were there. The first time I received a scratch on the right hip. We received orders to lie down, and fire, at least that is what we did. The balls then came like a hailstorm. I was soon struck the second time in the right hip inflicting a very severe wound, paralyzing both right limbs. Our troops then fell back, as many as could make their way back to our lines. I attempted it (using my gun as a staff or crutch) but fainted from the loss of blood but soon recovered, and found the woods all on fire. I lit a match as best I could, burned a space large enough to lie upon and thus escape the flames. This was quite a task for me in my weak condition. Two soldiers from Company C made their way to the spot and saved themselves. There we lay watching our poor wounded comrades burning to death. Such a horrible site I hope I may never see again. The two soldiers from Company C were Wm. Smythe and Henry Markle. Late on Monday evening we were carried out of the woods to an old log house where we lay on the ground without any shelter, but with little to eat and drink. It rained several times while we were there. One morning (May 4th) I lay in the water 6 inches deep unable to stir. A wounded man had rolled on me during the night I begged him to please roll away but he did not stir. After daybreak a Johnny came along and rolled him off and then I discovered that the man was dead. There were quite a number of dead horses lying around; the stench was almost unbearable."

After quoting from his letter, Young continued his narration in *The Story of Our Regiment,* his story relates some of the humanitarian feelings that were expressed between the opposing sides.

"The foregoing extract is not as explicit as it should be. The first volley fired into our ranks killed Samuel Leitzel on my right as he fell he struck me across the breast with his left hand. William Bible and Benjamin F Bloom in front of me, were also struck and both died from the wounds. Soon after the great fire had passed over, a squad of Confederate skirmishers passed us on at quick step and soon returned on the double quick, they never noticed us. An hour, or more perhaps, another squad of Johnnies in charge of a captain came along, they were unarmed and pretended they were looking after their wounded. They gathered around us, shook hands and told of Stonewall Jackson's death, expressed much sympathy on account of our suffering, bade us farewell as they saw their Captain approach. The Captain unlike his men was rude and gruff, he insultingly asked what we were doing here. I told him the only thing we could do was to lie here until somebody came to help us out. As he was about leaving I said, "Captain, I have shaken hands with every man that has been here this morning, and I want to shake with you." He came back, shook hands and left smiling. Night came on, it was a sad, dreary night for us. Comrade Markle was shot in the leg, from the effects of which he died about a month later. Comrade Smythe was shot through the lungs, the ball passing through his arm between the elbow and shoulder and then clean through the body. I met him several years later in Tiffin, Ohio, where he was running a grocery store. The bullet that hurt me most passed diagonally through the right hip shattering the hip bone. I mention this to give a faint idea of what a sad trio we were."

In the meantime, our enemy was positioning its artillery into position to rake us with grape-shot and canister so we were ordered to fall back, which we did. We set up a line of entrenchments which became our front, and which we held until the 5th of May. During the battle when the regiment was drawn up in line and before our company was put on the picket line, a stray shot would come towards us but no enemy would be in sight. Major Fairlamb was heard to ask William Perry, an old woodsman from Snow Shoe how he liked it. Perry was prompt with his response. "Well, Major, to stand here and be shot at and darsen't shoot back. I be dammed if I like it!" After our company found ourselves facing Fredericksburg on picket duty and employed as skirmishers, Perry and the rest of us solved the problem of not being able to shoot back.

On the fourth, our company was dug in in the center of the line facing the Confederates and we lost many good men. During this time period General Hooker had been dazed by a near miss of an artillery shell and most people in the know seemed to think that this incident severely affected his ability to lead his troops.

In the meantime Sedgwick had advanced from the east but was subsequently driven back by the rebel forces. By now it had become obvious that the battle had been lost. Despite a more than two to one advantage in men, Hooker had been severely out-generaled by Lee and the Union had suffered another defeat. Some people blamed Hooker's lack of generalship. Some people said that the near miss by the artillery shell had rendered him incapable of his decision making faculties. Others blamed what I referred to earlier as the "cowardice of the German troops in XI Corps." Who knows. It could have been a combination of some or all of the reasons given. The hard cold fact was that we had been beaten—badly beaten.

The only thing left for us to do was to recross the Rappahannock and retire to our camp at Falmouth. On the way back, a poor mule had become mired in the mud and there was really no chance of freeing her. She had sunk so far down that some of the men had used her back as a stepping stone. John English of our company saw her hopeless plight. He slipped a cartridge into his gun placed the muzzle against its ear, and put the poor creature out of its misery. Colonel McFarlane who had taken over the regiment in Colonel Beaver's absence came back and sought to find out who was responsible for this destruction of government property. Of course nobody volunteered any information and the colonel rode off to resume his duties as head of the regiment. We returned to our camp, chastened and much diminished by the unforgiving gods of war.

It had been our first battle and for much of the time we had been in the thick of the action. The rigorous training we had received from Col. Beaver stood us in good stead. Although we were a green regiment, our baptism of fire was such that we gained the respect of both the officers and experienced veterans with whom we served.

Chapter 8

The Aftermath of Chancellorsville

IT is hard to describe the feelings of remorse and depression that overcame us as we moved back into camp. As bad as it was for us, the situation in the Eleventh Corps was incalculably worse. We had all lost a battle, but the men of the Eleventh Corps had become the scapegoats and were blamed for our stunning defeat. The second of May had become a day that would live in infamy for them.

The Anglo-American newspapers wasted no time in blaming the Eleventh Corps for our defeat. They referred to it as the German Corps although there were many non-ethnic Germans in that corps. The newspapers were full of such expressions as "the Flying Dutchman" and "the damned Dutch." The newspapers, particularly those from New York, were full of articles stating that the Germans had turned tail and run, that they had left their weapons and all their belongings behind while charging to the rear, and many other inaccurate statements. These defamatory articles were quoted or reprinted throughout many cities in the north.

The newspapers were not alone. Many of the soldiers in the Army of the Potomac vented their frustrations on the German regiments, or on the Eleventh Corps as a whole. Many soldiers sent home letters totally blaming the Germans for our loss. Many of those letters found their way into newspapers and were published as fact. The truth is that many of those letters were written by soldiers who were not even close to where the action occurred and could not have witnessed what they claimed to have seen.

The generals who were really responsible in large part, were quick to join the chorus of those condemning the Germans. As stated earlier nativism was rampant throughout much of the country and the Army was no exception. Those people believed that anybody whose family had not lived in America for an extended period of time was suspect, lazy, cowardly and not to be trusted. After all they dressed differently, spoke a strange language that was totally incomprehensible and had very different customs. Not only that, they drank beer. This in and of itself was an anathema to many of the puritanical people who were given leadership roles in the Union Army. One of those people was the aforementioned General Howard who had just recently been given command of the Eleventh Corps. An example of his lack of understanding of the German culture and customs is the fact that he forbade the consumption of beer by his troops. This created great resentments, and if the truth be known, many of us non-Teutonic warriors also welcomed the arrival of beer wagons when they appeared on the scene.

Howard had just recently replaced General Sigel to whom his fellow German troops were particularly devoted. One of the phrases often quoted by many troops in the Army of the Potomac was "*ve fights mit Sigel.*" This phrase was used by many of the soldiers in a very derogatory manner and implied that the German soldiers would fight only under a German commander, and would not fight for an Anglo-American.

None of the commanders who filed reports or gave accounts to the newspapers mentioned the fact that many members of the German regiments brought to their commander's attention the fact that they had spotted Confederate movements to the right that appeared to be flanking the Eleventh Corps. Nor did they mention that these warnings were passed off and ignored as being unreliable, or in the alternative as being the movements of Confederate soldiers who were retreating.

These were but some of the many instances that brought such deep resentment and despair to the German soldiers, many of them had performed very well and were placed in an untenable position through no fault of their own.

Many of the German leaders and their soldiers attempted to remedy the inaccurate depictions of German cowardice by reporting the truth as they saw it to their own newspapers and attempting to counter the inaccurate and defamatory statements made in the press by both the reporters and many of the people involved in the battle. Unfortunately these articles and editorials were written in German and largely published only in the German press; thus were not available to the Anglo-Americans who had made the false accusations. Unfortunately the negative image of the German soldiers in the Army of the Potomac remained and affected the overall morale of the Army in a negative manner.

As a result of this unfortunate affair the reputation of Germans in the Army of the Potomac suffered throughout the war and their many acts of bravery and excellent soldiering were conveniently forgotten. Many people believe that the actions of the Anglo-American leaders had the effect of isolating and alienating the German soldiers fighting for the union cause. Also, many people believe these actions helped to unify the Germans who fought in our midst. This is a part of our history of which we should not be proud, but it happened.

Chapter 9

Back in Camp at Falmouth

B Y May sixth, we were back at our camp on the north side of the Rappahannock where we had built our winter quarters. The last ten days had been a trial for us. It was now time to regroup and to morn our losses. For our new regiment it was a bitter time. We had gone into battle with high hopes for a Union victory and returned diminished in numbers and spirit.

We did have one consolation. Many wounded men were saved who would have been lost had the battle been fought a year earlier. Our army, the Army of the Potomac, had made a major change at about the time our regiment had been organized. The Ambulance Corps had been added. They became guardian angels for men wounded in battle. Many a life was saved because of their work.

Prior to August of 1862, rescue and care of the wounded on the battlefield had been left to non-combatants and was not always efficiently or competently carried out. Quite often this task was left to the bandsmen who worked diligently although they were often not trained or equipped to carry out these duties. Also other non-combatants who held their positions because they were not particularly good as soldiers were thrust into that role. It goes without saying that a man who is not a good soldier is not going to be good at rescuing the wounded from the battlefield. Many a poor soul who could have been saved left this life lying on the field of battle where he had been struck down by an enemy ball. If there had been someone to administer first aid and get him to a hospital quickly he might have lived to tell about his part in the great struggle to save our Union.

On August second, 1862, General McClellan issued an order that established the Ambulance Corps. Jonathan Letterman who was the medical director of the Army of the Potomac developed a plan known as the Letterman Ambulance Plan. The ambulances of a given division moved together under the command of a mounted line sergeant with two stretcher-bearers and a driver for each ambulance. Their duty was to collect wounded from the battle as soon as possible and transport them to dressing stations and field hospitals. This greatly improved care of the wounded.

I have been told that the Quartermaster Corps did not like this plan at all. They had previously been in control of the ambulances and they hated losing their control. Some of the field commanders were also notable for their noncooperation. Perhaps those opponents never had to watch our poor wounded boys, left dying on the field unattended.

That being said, it is still true that a great many of our brave young men who had been wounded died on the battlefield. This was especially true at Chancellorsville and the subsequent battles of the Wilderness and Spotsylvania. These battles were largely fought in extremely dense brush and undergrowth. The forests which had once blanketed the area had long since been harvested as fuel for the many iron furnaces in the area. The terrain was almost impenetrable because of the new growth which had sprung up where the forests had been. It was a mass of young trees and brambles which made horse drawn transportation next to impossible.

These three battles could have been named Wilderness One, Wilderness Two and Wilderness Three. The land over which we fought was much the same in each of these battles. One tragic result of the dense growth was that the explosions of shells as well as the flames produced by the rifles caught the woods on fire. The dense smoke and flames made rescue of our wounded impossible and they died horrible deaths. For years after, the skeletal remains of these unfortunate warriors could be found lying where they had fallen.

As our army paused to repair itself and to regain its strength, it was very important to keep an eye on our adversary situated on the far bank of the Rappahannock. Although there was some talk about proceeding on to Richmond, nobody really knew what was in the mind of our opponent, General Lee. Our army's intelligence sent out spies and our pickets were ever on the lookout for movement by the enemy. No one seemed to know what was happening. The reader must remember that I was a corporal and like the rest of the army did not have any knowledge of the Confederate intentions, let alone our own plans or movements. As you can imagine, it is the people who actually fight the battles who are the last to know what is happening, where and when. As for that matter our own leaders had no idea of Lee's plans or movements. I must remind the reader that much of what appears in this little book is information I gained after the war from my comrades in arms or the writings of the Generals or from accounts published in newspapers at the time they happened.

Tracking the movements of the enemy was a job generally entrusted to the cavalry. If they failed in their duty all could be lost. They were quite often referred to as the eyes and ears of the Army.

As the Union forces were resting and regaining strength, Lee had already started to move his forces in a northwesterly direction. On June third the confederate forces had quietly withdrawn from around Fredericksburg, leaving A. P. Hill's corps in the fortifications around Fredericksburg to act as a decoy and rear guard. Two days later the Confederate forces under Longstreet and Ewell had advanced the forty or so miles to the vicinity of Culpepper. The leader of our army, General Hooker, figured out that Lee was on the move and the events of the next month have become known as the "Gettysburg Campaign." Keep in mind that, as was generally the case, the soldiers in the field had no idea where we were headed and that the decisive battle of the war would be contested at Gettysburg in less than a month.

During that month the Union army moved approximately 90,000 men and the Confederates moved about 75,000 men well over a hundred miles and fought five or six battles. Of course our regiment, the 148th Pennsylvania, was not involved in all these actions, but it is important for people to know the tremendous scope of what happened during that momentous month. To illustrate the scope of this movement and of the battle to come; if you read this book from cover to cover you will have read fewer than half as many words as there were people contesting that great battle.

Chapter 10

On the Road to Gettysburg

OUR regiment remained in camp around Falmouth till the fourteenth of June when we were finally ordered north. We were under the command of Lieutenant Colonel McFarlane. Colonel E. E. Cross of the 5th New Hampshire had been commanding the brigade. There was no love lost between our men and Colonel Cross. For some reason he had taken a distinct dislike of our regiment and took every opportunity to heap insults upon the regiment in the absence of our recently wounded leader, Colonel Beaver. We could not understand why an officer and, supposedly, a gentleman could act that way, unless he had become jealous of our superior appearance and deportment in battle. We were forced to endure his insults and derogatory comments in silence, and we hated him. We hated Colonel Beaver, too, in the beginning but we came to respect and even love him because we learned that he exemplified everything that an officer and a gentleman should be.

Colonel Beaver had transformed us from a rag tag bunch of students, farm boys and woodsmen into a fighting unit that we believed to be second to none. Many of the men have a firm conviction that the training they received and the spirit he instilled in us literally saved their lives in many a battle. Our judgment of him as a fine and capable man was certainly proven correct later, as he was eventually elected governor of our great state.

As stated above, the Second Corps of which we were a part moved out from Falmouth on the fourteenth of June. Although Hooker knew a week before that Lee was on the move, we were unable to move any earlier. With ninety thousand troops to move, and roads that were not the best or the most numerous it took a certain amount of time and much planning to set the army in motion.

We started our trek northwards, not knowing where we were headed, marching through the towns of Stafford, Dumfries, and Centerville. We crossed the sight of the Battles of Bull Run and that was a truly gruesome sight. Many of the fallen from those battles had been buried in shallow graves and the remains of many soldiers who had fallen lay at least partially exposed. You could always tell which of the bodies had been Johnny Reb's and which had been from our side. The confederate boys were all laid out with their heads pointing to the south, while ours were largely oriented in the opposite direction. There was no light-hearted banter among the troops as we trudged through those fields of death and destruction. The memory of that sight hangs heavy on my mind to this day, as I am sure it does for many a man who passed by that way. Who can say which is worse, the horrors of battle, or the aftermath? In the heat of battle there is no time for reflection; you just do what you do. Marching past those fallen comrades you have time to think—"That could have been me."

Other pesky things also kept us occupied as we trudged along in the early summer heat, with our heavy packs and our sweaty woolen uniforms. It was on that march that many of us were first invaded by that universal enemy of all soldiers in the field, those evil creatures known by our men as "greybacks." You might better know them as the body louse. When they descended upon you it was first by the squad, then the company, followed shortly by the regiment, the brigade and finally by the whole division. I was first invaded around the twenty-first of June when we had reached Thoroughfare Gap, and where we rested for a few days. At about that time there was an issue of clothing by the Quartermaster and I bought an entire set of clothes. Every stitch of clothing, including my blanket, found its way to the camp fire double quick step. Thankfully that was the last time I suffered from such an invasion.

On June twenty-six it was back on the march and we passed through Gum Springs, Edwards Ferry, Poolsville, Sugar Loaf Mountain and Frederick City, reaching Uniontown in the evening of the thirtieth. This is where our regiment received its ultimate insult. Colonel Cross, mentioned earlier, relieved Lt. Colonel McFarlane from command of our regiment and placed Colonel McKeen of the 81st Pennsylvania in command of the 148th. This was a totally uncalled for and unjustified action on the part of Colonel Cross. Our men were livid but there was nothing we could do to change this intolerable act. It was not that Colonel McKeen was not an able leader. He was. It was that this small minded and unfair officer had used his authority to vilify and disgrace a good officer and an outstanding regiment in order to feed some unknown personal animus. There was much angry talk at our campsite that evening. Little did we know that justice would be served and Colonel Cross would receive a just and lasting reward in just a few days hence.

"READY, ALWAYS READY"

Of course, as history has recorded, Colonel McFarlane was not the only officer to be relieved at this same time. Hooker, in a fit of pique, offered his resignation to President Lincoln. To General Hooker's complete surprise, it was promptly accepted and General Meade was immediately named to be the commander of the Army of the Potomac. As a result of his actions at Chancellorsville, Hooker had earned the reputation of being too defensive minded. Thus continued the dance of musical chairs at the top of the Army of the Potomac—first Burnside, then Hooker and now Meade. Had we won a battle things might have been different.

Inside of a week our new commander would face the challenge of a lifetime. Until June 28, Meade had been the commander of the Fifth Corps. Now he was suddenly thrust into the leadership of an army that was starved for a victory. The Army of the Potomac had established a reputation—superior in numbers, inferior in leadership. It was now up to Meade to change that reputation.

It is important to remember that almost a month passed from the time Lee's forces left their camp around Fredericksburg until the great battle of Gettysburg. Several actions were fought as the two great armies moved north. The 148th was not involved, but I will give you a brief account of actions that occurred before that great clash at the beginning of July.

On June ninth, Lee had ordered his cavalry under the famed J. E.B. Stuart to cross the Rappahannock in order to screen his army from being observed by the Union forces as it moved north. The Union cavalry under Pleasanton met the Confederate forces at Brandy Station. This proved to be the biggest cavalry battle ever fought in America. That battle was considered more or less a draw although Stuart claimed victory for the rebel forces.

Lee's Army headed across the Blue Ridge Mountains to head north down the Shenandoah Valley. On June the fourteenth the second battle of Winchester took place. It was a disaster for us. We suffered almost 4,500 casualties, 4,000 of which were captured. By comparison the Confederates lost only 250. We were to the east of the Confederate forces as we moved north. Part of our job was to be sure we were interspersed between the Confederates and Washington D.C., which we did. Also we did not even start our trek north till the fourteenth so our regiment suffered little more than hot sweaty marches along the dusty roads, as well as the aforementioned pesky "greyback invasions."

"READY, ALWAYS READY"

Chapter 11

Prelude to Gettysburg

AT the end of June as Lee's army had crossed over from Maryland into Pennsylvania, Stuart had crossed over to the east of the Union forces and was consequently no longer able to provide the eyes or cover for Lee's army. By the twenty-ninth of June his army was spread out in an arc from Chambersburg to Carlisle, Pennsylvania and on to an area near Harrisburg. If he could take Camp Curtain at Harrisburg it would surely be a feather in his camp and it might help the undermanned and out supplied Confederate forces actually win the war. However, he was informed by a spy in the employ of General Longstreet that the Union forces had crossed the Potomac and were, uncharacteristically, in hot pursuit.

He immediately ordered his forces to concentrate at Cashtown. This was located about nine or tem miles east and slightly north of Gettysburg. On June thirtieth, one of Hill's brigades of North Carolinians advanced in the direction of Gettysburg. Some people claim they were out searching for supplies, particularly shoes. This is entirely possible because our Southern adversaries were not at all well-equipped, and many of the Confederate soldiers had very old, worn out shoes or no shoes at all. As they were approaching town they spotted Union cavalry arriving south of town. They immediately returned to Cashtown and reported what they saw.

Lee had issued orders for his troops to avoid a general engagement until he could get all of his troops concentrated in one place. In spite of this order, Hill decided to mount what was called " a reconnaissance in force." The next day at five o'clock in the morning, Hill ordered two brigades to advance on Gettysburg. The battle was about to begin.

As those brigades were advancing towards Gettysburg, they were met first by dismounted cavalrymen under General Buford of our forces. The cavalrymen fought a delaying action while the troops of the First Corps under General Reynolds could get into position.

In the meantime, our regiment along with the rest of the Second Corps was still at Uniontown, a village on the Maryland side of the Pennsylvania/ Maryland border, twenty-three miles southeast of Gettysburg. We had begun the march northwards, reaching Taneytown at about noon. From Taneytown we headed on up to Gettysburg, still eleven miles away. As strenuous as this march was, our comrades in the Sixth Corps were forced to cover over thirty miles on a forced march to get to the site of the battle. Remember, this was the first of July and we endured a punishing full day's march in the summer heat before we could even get to the battle.

Fatigue meant little to us on this day. We were back in Pennsylvania and had come home to defend our land against an enemy who was intent on tearing our nation asunder. We were fighting for the Union on our home ground!

Chapter 12

The Battle of Gettysburg

THE two Confederate brigades of Heth's Division from Hill's Corps had come forward to Gettysburg and had been met by the dismounted cavalrymen. This was a vital action because the bulk of the Union forces had yet to arrive on the scene. They held on valiantly until the rest of the Union forces began to arrive.

The First Corps, commanded by General Reynolds, came on to the scene from south of Gettysburg and met the enemy, repulsing the Confederate assaults which had come down the Chambersburg Pike. Unfortunately for the Union cause, General Reynolds became an early casualty as he was killed at this early stage of the battle.

The Eleventh Corps which had arrived on the scene was the next Union force to enter the fray. The Federal forces positioned themselves in a semicircular position from west to the north of town. The Confederates attacked in force and the Union line held under extreme pressure. Finally after being attacked from both the north and the west the Union lines broke and were forced to withdraw through the town, taking many casualties and losing many prisoners. Remember, this was the same Eleventh Corps who had been so vilified after the battle of Chancellorsville. On this day, as on many others, they fought bravely in spite of the exhausting march they had endured to arrive at Gettysburg.

After withdrawing south through the town our forces established good defensive positions on the high ground at Cemetery Hill and waited for further attacks. Lee had ordered his forces under General Ewell to attack the Union forces in their defensive position if practicable but an expected attack from the Confederate forces never materialized. This ended the first day of battle.

All during that first day of battle we marched forward to Gettysburg but we did not know where we were headed and, strangely enough, heard none of the noise of battle. Our regiment had no knowledge of the terrible battle being fought until the ambulance bearing the body of General Reynolds who had fallen early on passed by our troops as it was taken to the rear.

That evening as darkness was gathering around us, and as we approached within two miles of Gettysburg, General Hancock, our Corps commander placed us in line on the Taneytown road. We were placed in this position so that we would be able to support either the right or left flank of the line, whichever place we were needed. We stayed there till morning of the second when after a careful inspection of our weapons we moved forward and advanced to the field. Our second Corps never actually arrived at the battlefield till about eight in the morning when we were placed into line.

As you might imagine getting a force of 90,000 men plus artillery and supplies to the site of a battle and placing all the various units in position at the proper place and at the right time was an almost insurmountable task. In spite of this, our new leader General Meade was up to the job.

As our generals became aware of where the rebel lines were developing, the Second Corps was moved to the west and became the left of our line along Cemetery Ridge. We were facing the rebel forces who had gathered in front of us on Seminary Ridge. Our regiment was on the left of our line along with the rest of our division. As we lay in our position waiting for the action to start, each man was left with his own thoughts. We were on Pennsylvania soil defending our land. Nobody among us knew who would live to see another day.

We heard the rumble of moving artillery, some sporadic cannon fire and occasional rattling of musket fire off to the right. Other than that it was relatively quiet. Sometime in the middle of the day there appeared a large column of Union infantry marching south at right angles to us down the road that intersected Taneytown Road. We soon figured out that this was General Sickle's Third Corps. They marched right past our line and forward to the high ground along the Emmitsburg Road. That road ran obliquely in a northeasterly direction until it intersected with the Taneytown Road at the south edge of Gettysburg.

He positioned his troops with great precision. His right was facing west along the road to the now famous peach orchard and his left curving from the peach orchard to the Devil's Den in front of Little Round Top. There was a problem, however. His right was several hundred yards in front of our left and this created a huge gap in the line. Totally unknown to us was the fact that Sickles had disregarded Meade's orders and had positioned his troops far in advance of where he had been ordered. Sickles was known as an aggressive General, but in this case his aggressiveness could have very easily cost us the battle, as it turns out. He was also not known to suffer criticism lightly, and he spent the remainder of his life trying to convince anyone who would listen that his judgment had been right and Meade had been wrong. Sickles claimed that Meade's plan was not sufficiently aggressive, was too timid, and that he had in fact prepared orders for the Union army to withdraw at the slightest sign of trouble. This assertion was not borne out by the facts, in spite of Sickles lifelong contentions to the contrary.

We were not the only people who were aware of the Third Corps position. Our opponent, General Longstreet was aware and had begun his movement towards our lines. His march was well hidden from our view by the dense woods and ridges west of the Emmitsburg Road. It wasn't until afternoon that Longstreet's forces commenced the fight. They attacked the far left of our line which ran northeasterly from Little Round Top and Devil's Den. They were advancing like a wave, starting at the extreme left wing and gradually moving north.

As the Confederate troops moved in a northwesterly direction they were at first unaware that it was the entire Third Corps under Sickles which had advanced beyond the rest of the Union forces. Troops from Georgia and Arkansas moved through and into the Wheatfield which would henceforth give its name to this bloody part of the Gettysburg Battle. As they entered the Wheatfield they encountered the Union Brigades from the Third Corps. Burling's Brigade from the Third Corps withdrew into the safety of Trostle's Woods. Trostle's Woods was away from our line (that is, in front of our position) and that created a bigger gap in the Line.

Soldiers from Georgia tried to enter the gap but were caught in a cross fire from both sides of the gap. We also saw hand to hand fighting at a stone wall near the edge of Rose's Woods. The rebels withdrew into the safety of Rose's Woods and the Wheatfield remained in our hands—for now. I should add that although we could see the action from our vantage point it was not always possible to identify the individual units involved. If a person could not identify the unit by its colors it was necessary to find out after the fact through comrades or from newspapers or other sources which would eventually be available. As I already mentioned, much of the information in this book has come from my fellow soldiers or from articles written at the time. There are several things that the common soldier in the field hardly ever knows—where he had been, where he was now and where he was going.

Late in the afternoon the Confederates renewed their advance into the Wheatfield, but this time with additional forces. All the Union troops were being forced to withdraw under the heavy Confederate attack and they eventually took control of the Wheatfield. All of Sickles troops who had advanced to the Wheatfield, contrary to Meade's orders, had by now withdrawn from the fighting. Help was desperately needed and this is when our division was called into action.

Our Brigade under Colonel Cross was the first to enter the fray in the Wheatfield. We were followed by General Zook and then by the Irish Brigade. Our regiment was among the first to engage the enemy. As we advanced, we steadily drove the enemy back. Under heavy fire, we continued to drive the enemy, but were taking heavy casualties in killed and wounded. Ammunition was running low and we were forced to retire as evening settled in on the battlefield. Our regiment and the 5th New Hampshire held their positions till the last cartridge had expired and remained in position until relieved by a brigade from the Fifth Corps. Colonel McKeen made special mention of this detachment in his report. Every last man in our unit held fast unless wounded or killed until we were relieved. It was at this battle that I injured my left leg.

Darkness brought an end to the day's struggle. The Wheatfield became a no man's land for the time being, not occupied by either side. The Union line had held. Sickles had paid for his over aggressive actions, taken contrary to the orders given by Meade, with a leg. Colonel Cross who had treated our regiment so badly suffered a more severe fate. The temperature at Gettysburg was very hot during the battle, but Cross had left us, to dwell in a place much, much hotter than Gettysburg in July. The men of the 148th Pennsylvania Volunteers did not particularly mourn his passing.

That night we slept with heavy hearts, grieving for our comrades who would never awaken from their slumbers. July third found us placed along Cemetery Ridge at Emmitsburg Road. General Hancock ordered us to fortify our positions as well as possible with whatever was at hand. We worked furiously constructing defenses from earth and anything else at hand. By the end of the morning there was not a fence rail to be seen in the vicinity. As it turned out, our efforts were very well spent.

Fighting started early in the morning to our right as our troops sought to retake the lower slopes of Culp's hill which had been lost the previous day. After many hours of hard fighting, our Union lines were intact. We watched as the Confederates massed their artillery on Seminary Ridge. Our forces could not place as many pieces facing the Confederates to our west, simply because our line was much shorter and there was no room for more guns.

Sometime shortly after noon a tremendous artillery barrage got under way. We did not know why, but our guns were not answering in reply. Those who could not observe the placement of our batteries were afraid that the gunners from south of the Mason-Dixon Line had bested our boys and knocked our guns out of action. What those of us who did not have clear sight lines did not know, was that the rebel cannon had been aimed too high and many overshot their intended targets. As the day progressed, however, our artillerymen proved their mettle.

Lee had planned to begin the assault on the Union line at Cemetery Ridge earlier in the day but Longstreet's troops had not gotten into position early enough. It was at three in the afternoon when we witnessed a sight that none of us will ever forget. Out of the woods north of the Peach Orchard came over twelve-thousand of the Confederate troops to attack the center of our line! They whooped and hollered and shouted as they advanced along the field, determined to win another victory for the cause of the south. This was the momentous event that would forever be known as "Picket's Charge" and was the single event that marked the beginning of the end for the Confederacy.

They had three quarters of a mile to travel before reaching our lines, and with their colors flying and their officers urging them on it was an awesome sight. They charged forward, breaking into a run. Suddenly Union artillery opened fire on our battle crazed foes with ball and canister. Many of the rebel yells were replaced by shrieks and screams of agony, but still they came. Our batteries continued to rain death and destruction upon them. Their ranks grew thin, but still they came. They had formed an oblique line and were headed straight for our position.

Finally—they were within musket range. We opened up with our Springfields. Grey and butternut clad soldiers fell—more screams—more rebel yells—more blood. Still they came. Still they fell. A vanguard of their brave warriors reached our line at a little copse of woods and for a moment our boys in blue wavered and there was hand to hand fighting but victory for the sons of the south would not be theirs this day. Our boys regrouped and stood fast where the line had wavered. Many of the Confederate soldiers saw the hopelessness of their struggle. They threw down their weapons and crossed over our lines into captivity as prisoners of war.

One of Picket's leading generals was Lewis Armistead. He and General Hancock were best friends and had served together before the war. When the war broke out he, like General Lee, felt compelled to join the Confederate Army. So it was that two good friends faced each other in battle at Gettysburg. Armistead lead at the head of his troops and reached the Union line. When the Union soldiers launched a counterattack, Armistead was shot three times and mortally wounded.

As he lay bleeding, his first thoughts were of his friend Hancock. He was told that Hancock had also been wounded and he said "Not both of us the same day!" Hancock could not go to comfort his good friend because of the injuries he himself had suffered. Two days later Armistead died from his wounds and one of his dying wishes was that his personal effects and his Bible go to his longtime friend, General Hancock.

General Longstreet set down some of his observations of that famous charge in an article appearing in *Battles and Leaders of the Civil War* some twenty years after Gettysburg. In that article, he stated that he had objected to the assault but had been overruled by Lee. Here is some of what he wrote.

"That day at Gettysburg was one of the saddest of my life. I foresaw what my men would meet and would gladly have given up my position rather than share in the responsibilities of that day. It was thus I felt when Pickett at the head of 4,900 brave men marched over the crest of Seminary Ridge and began his descent of the slope. As he passed me he rode gracefully, with his jaunty cap raked well over his right ear and his long auburn locks, nicely dressed, hanging almost to his shoulders. He seemed rather a holiday soldier than a general at the head of a column which was about to make one of the grandest, most desperate assaults recorded in the annals of wars. Armistead and Garnett, two of his brigadiers, were veterans of nearly a quarter of a century's service. Their minds seemed absorbed in the men behind, and in the bloody work before them. Kemper, the other brigadier, was younger but had experienced many severe battles. He was leading my old brigade that I had drilled on Manassas plains before the first battle on that noted field. The troops advanced in well-closed ranks and with elastic steps, their faces lighted with hope. ... As soon as Pickett passed the crest of the hill, the Federals had a clear view and opened their batteries, and as he descended the eastern slope of the ridge his troops received a fearful fire from the batteries in front and from Round Top. The troops marched steadily, taking the fire with great coolness. ... The slaughter was terrible, the enfilade fire of the batteries on Round

"READY, ALWAYS READY"

Top being very destructive. At times one shell would knock down five or six men. [Colonel Freemantle had been watching with Longstreet] ... Colonel Freemantle, only observing the troops of Pickett's command said to me 'General, I would not have missed this for anything in the world.' He believed it to be a complete success. I was watching the troops supporting Pickett and saw plainly they could not hold together all ten minutes longer. I called his attention to the wavering condition of the two divisions of the Third Corps, and said they would not hold, that Pickett would be crushed and the attack would be a failure."

As is well known today, General Longstreet's assessment was totally accurate. The high watermark of the Confederacy had come and gone.

During the battle of Gettysburg, the Union losses and casualties were approximately 30,000 out of a force of 90,000. Proportionately our foes suffered even greater losses; 27,000 out a total force of 75,000. The next day was Independence Day, July fourth, the eighty-seventh anniversary of the founding of our fractured country. The Union had prevailed in what proved to be the pivotal battle of the war, but there was no time to celebrate and no time to mourn. We had to bury our dead, tend to our wounded and march on.

Chapter 13

The Pioneers at Gettysburg

A S I mentioned earlier, the pioneers were a very important part of our regiment. I detailed earlier their duties on the march and in camp. They were strong and rugged men who did whatever was asked of them. At Gettysburg they assumed monumental tasks. Sgt. Thomas Meyer wrote the Pioneer's story in *The Story of Our Regiment.* It is a detailed story and gives a very good description of the pioneers and how they performed. The following is his description of the pioneers and their actions at the Battle of Gettysburg. I will let him take up the story starting when they bivouacked just four miles from Gettysburg at 9:00 PM on July first, in the evening of the first day of battle.

"We were now close up to the Confederate Army. We realized that we were upon the field of an impending great battle. The battle had already commenced. During the day, though we could not hear the noise of battle, we saw the white powder smoke of battle rise in great clouds far away to the northward and drift slowly along on the light breeze. The boys became quite meditative. We stacked arms, threw off knapsacks, accoutrements and coats, and commenced building a parapet along our front. The sky cleared and the moon shone brightly. The pioneers felled the trees and the troops carried and placed them in position. The gray dawn of coming day tinged the eastern horizon, when we pronounced our work finished.

Early on the morning of July second, after a hurried lunch of crackers only, we filed out of our position and marched forward rapidly. About three miles toward Gettysburg, when we reached the battlefield and were assigned, a position in the great line of battle, seven miles long, on the now historic "Field of Gettysburg," near the "Clump of Trees" and the point now known as the "Bloody Angle." The Confederates on Seminary Ridge discovered our approaching columns, kept up vigorous shell fire on us during the last mile's march.

Squads of frightened citizens, men, women and children, carrying bandboxes and packages of hastily gathered valuables, who had abandoned their homes between the lines, and were running by us to find places of safety to our rear. One party, passing right along our column, consisted of an old gentleman leading a little girl by the hand on each side, and two young ladies carrying bandboxes, one also leading a child, running close by me. I said, "Good Morning, father." He gloomily responded. I said "Fine morning." He answered, "Yes truly, but so full of terror and sorrow;" tears were in his eyes as he raised his hand toward our column and said, "God bless and spare you all." Again they ran. Just as they passed our point in the rapidly moving column when a twenty-four pound rifle shell came screaming through the air and exploded with a frightful report over them. I looked back to see if they had escaped; the two ladies had fallen. After some effort they regained to their feet and ran faster than before, apparently all right. They had been knocked down by the force of the concussion only.

According to orders received at eleven o'clock at night, I took the pioneers of the Regiment, with pics, shovels and sperm candles, back to an open air field hospital, behind a rocky bluff, a mile to our right rear where several thousand wounded had been carried during the day while the battle was in progress, to sort the dead from the living and to bury them. We reached the hospital designated and found acres of ground covered with wounded, and among them, many who died after being brought here from the field. The pioneers of the 148th were the only men on duty at this point during the night.

We lit our candles and examined the situation. It was an awful place. The most able writer could not give the slightest shadow of an idea of this dreadful charnel scene; the awful sites in the Wheatfield and Death Valley thickly strewn over with weapons, cannons, broken gun carriages, thousands of dead men and horses, mutilated in all manner of form and degree, when we left it in the early evening was incomparable behind this scene of suffering and death. Here the dead and wounded lay promiscuously side by side, and close together, in long rows, on the bare wet ground, the feet of one row nearly touching the heads of the next row, the Union and Confederate in separate rows.

All was darkness; not a torch or candle burning. For some unknown reason, there were no surgeons in attendance on the wounded at this place during this night, at least not from midnight to 3:00 AM, during which time we were at work there; yet about half of them had their wounds dressed, lying on the bare ground, un-sheltered, uncovered, many of them nearly naked. Here the men in hundreds of oases dressed each other's wounds, making bandages out of their drawers taken from their bodies for the purpose. Many a soldier gave drawers and a shirt from his body to bandage the wounds of his comrades. Men wounded in the legs had the pant legs cut off, some close to the body, leaving the leg entirely naked; in the same way arms, chest, all parts of the body naked and uncovered. There were no blankets or tents, absolutely nothing. Many lay entirely helpless in the scorching sun and rain until the skin was scalded and burned into peeling blisters in the faces, and worse in parts of the body, tender and unaccustomed to exposure to the sun.

We found, by the dim light of our sperm candles, many of the 148th boys. Some had their wounds dressed and were sleeping soundly. Among them Amos Ehrhardt, of Company A, like the rest, few clothes, no cover, with a nasty hole through the thigh just gracing the femur artery; the pant leg cut off at the body, shoe and stocking gone, the naked leg as cold as ice, his head much lower than his body, the wound was nicely dressed and not bleeding. He was sleeping quietly, and as soundly as anyone could in the best bed. I put a flat stone under his head to put him in a more comfortable position and stop the rattle in his throat. Manassas Gilbert, also of company A, was found here sitting on the ground with his back against a tree, with the bullet in his shoulder, but wide-awake. Deep moans of agony in continuous chorus, were heard, but in all this vast number of desperately wounded men there was not a tear or a single noisy outcry.

Some of my men carried out the dead and laid them in rows, heads all one way, and one against the other. About the third man carried out was the tyrant commander of our brigade, Col. Cross of the fifth New Hampshire Regiment, killed in the woods near the Wheatfield. We did not bury him. Some of the men buried the dead and thus laid in rows; a shallow grave about a foot deep, against the first man in a row, and he was laid down into it; a similar grave was dug where he had lain. The ground thus dug up served to cover the first man, and the second man was laid in a trench, and so on, so the ground was handled only once. This was the regular form of burial on our battlefield; it is the most rapid, and is known as trench burial, and is employed where time for work is limited.

At about three o'clock in the morning, our candles were all burned up and we returned to a similar field hospital, just to the rear of our division battle lines, with about twelve hundred wounded here we lay down for a short rest; we had had little chance for rest or sleep day or night for two weeks, and we were very much fatigued.

Here the wounded seem to be in greater distress. The endless and louder moans were indicative of intense suffering. The voice of a boy was heard in prolonged loud wails and screams, high above the rest. His voice became horse and husky, but as morning came he was more quiet, and a little later entirely still. I imagined he had fallen asleep. As soon as it was light enough I went over and asked the wounded lying near, "Where is the boy that was in such agony during the night?" A wounded soldier raised himself on his elbow, pointed over a few others and said, "That is him; He Is Now Dead." I went over to him. He was a boy about sixteen, smooth faced as a woman and handsome. He was dead; one of his feet was torn into an unrecognizable mass of flesh, bone and sinew. Gangrene was evidently the immediate cause of death. Early amputation would have saved the boy's life. Here many had died of their unattended wounds during the night.

Many of the badly wounded were chloroformed to have their wounds dressed. When the operations were finished they were carried away, and laid out on the ground there was no time to assist them in resuscitation, and many never woke again. Many strangled to death for the want of a little assistance at the proper time.

July 3rd: the Pioneer corps held a council of war, and decided that it was preferable to fight with our respective companies rather than in the rear of the colors, so we disbanded and joined our companies for the balance of the fight."

I doubt that few if any could tell the story of the pioneers, their duties and experiences any better than Sgt. Meyer. His honest and straightforward narration is unequaled and stands as a living testimony of the horrors of this great war. Meyer continued his narration and told about the battlefield as the men resumed their duties of Pioneer at the conclusion of the battle.

"On the morning of July fourth, according to orders, I reassembled my pioneers and took them out on the field of Pickett's charge and fight to bury the dead. The field presented a dreadful site; the dead were already in a terrible state of putrefaction. Faces black as charcoal and bloated out of all humans semblance; eyes, cheeks, forehead and nose all on one general level of putrid swelling, twice the normal size with here and there great blisters of putrid water, some the size of a man's fist on face, neck and wrists; while the bodies were bloated to the full capacity of the uniforms that enclosed them.

It was a rare occurrence to find one who had not been robbed by the battlefield bandit or robber of the dead. Generally their pockets were cut open and rifled through the incision. The battlefield robbers were well known by the large amounts of money they had, and the watches, pocketbooks, pocket knives, and other valuable trinkets they had for sale after the battle. All regiments had them.

First we collected the dead men into rows, as usual, laying one against the other, heads all one way, Union and Confederate in separate rows. Then some would collect and arrange in rows while the majority of men buried them in trenches as heretofore described. These burial trenches were dug here, there and everywhere over the field and contained three or four or 50 as the number of dead nearby required. Few of these men had anything about them by which they could be identified, and they were buried as "unknown."

The Confederates still (July 4th) had sharpshooters in the trees beyond the Emmitsburg Road, and several times during the day they drove us off the field. The day was hot, sultry with frequent heavy showers. The stench of the battlefield was something indescribable, it would come up as if in waves and when at its worst the breath would stop in the throat; the lungs could not take it in, and a sense of suffocation would be experienced. We would cover our faces tightly with our hands and turn the back toward the breeze and wretch and gasped for breath.

The dead were found in all manner of positions, lying, sitting, isolated, in groups, in heaps. Many there were without a visible wound or mark to cause death. Down beyond the "Bloody Angle" there remained standing a few panels of post fence, only the lower rails remaining. Against this; a smooth faced soldier boy was sitting, his elbow resting on the second rail, his head resting on his right hand, his head upright the face turn toward us. Thinking he was sick or wounded I went out to offer assistance, and found he was dead. We examined him and found he had been shot through the left breast in the hand to hand fight at the "Bloody Angle" with Picket's men the day before, then sat down just as we found him and died without a struggle. There was nothing about him by which he could be identified. His accoutrements were still all in place, his cartridge box nearly empty.

One young soldier wounded under the arm asked the surgeon to address his wound; he could not raise his arm. The surgeon took all of his hand and jerked it violently up and a handful of big maggots fell out. Here occurred one of the most pathetic incidents of the war. A young soldier, a mere boy who was brought to the hospital carried on a stretcher while a soldier walked alongside and with his hand held the wound in the thigh near the body. He said he was entirely free from pain. A surgeon examined the wound and said, "Nothing can be done for you; you must die; if you have any word or message to send home, attend to it at once; you will die within a few moments after your comrade takes his hand from your wound and that must be soon." He asked for paper and pen which were quickly furnished. He wrote a letter to his mother, stated his condition and that a comrade was holding the wound while he wrote to her, saying that as soon as he finished the letter his comrade would let go and he would bleed to death in a few minutes. The letter was finished, he let himself fall back, hesitated a moment, then said, "Now you may let go," and Levi Smith, of Company A, 148th, who held the wound withdrew his hand, and in a few minutes life had gone out."

Matthew Brady, the photographer, became famous for the photographs he took on the battlefield. When a person looks at these photos it is impossible to really understand or see the aftermath of the battles as we saw and experienced them.

Chapter 14

Aftermath of Gettysburg

AS has already been described by Sgt. Meyer, the battlefield it-self on the morning of July fourth was a vision straight from hell. Dead and wounded soldiers were lying everywhere. The dead were lying in every conceivable position, some stacked in piles with arms and legs akimbo, others with limbs missing, headless torsos and corpses with frightful wounds. Others lay peacefully on the ground as though asleep. The moans and cries of the wounded were heart wrenching—young men calling out for their mothers or their sweethearts—some just begging for water.

There was blood everywhere. The brave men of the Ambulance Corps as well as musicians and other noncombatants were real heroes on that day. They tended to the wounded as best they could; adminis-tering what aid and comfort they could and transporting them by stretcher or ambulance to the various aid stations and field hospitals. There were temporary hospitals set up throughout the periphery of the battlefield, some in private residences. They could easily be recog-nized by the piles of amputated arms and legs that rapidly grew outside the windows of the makeshift hospitals as the surgeons went about their grizzly work.

Human suffering was not the only sorrowful thing to be wit-nessed. Dead horses dotted the landscape, as many of the unfortunate beasts who had hauled the artillery and carted the supplies were not exempt from the carnage. Some of the poor wounded creatures stag-gered or crawled about, their miserable cries rending the air. There were so many of them that some of our men were given the unpleasant duty of putting them out of their misery. The stench of dead and dying was everywhere.

For our survivors, there was no victory celebration. We had marched for days over long distances reaching Gettysburg in the nick of time to enter into battle with an enemy who was intent on inflicting another defeat on the Union forces. We were dead tired. Our heavy woolen uniforms were soaked through with our own sweat from the toils and heavy exertion in the hot summer sun. We had lost many comrades to the gods of war; some of them had been lifelong friends.

There were many who had no rest at all after reaching Gettysburg, and were thrown into battle as soon as they reached the site. Many of them were what was known as stragglers. They were not malingerers and were not at fault. As we marched along, headed for we knew not where, some of the men became ill or became so fatigued that when they sat down for a little rest they immediately dozed off. By the time they had awakened from their unintended slumbers the units had moved on, so they were forced to struggle along behind the main force hoping to find their comrades. Some were just too sick to move and they were left behind, hopefully to reunite with their units later. This was not a small problem. Some people say that illness took as many lives as battle. This was the 1860's. Sanitation and medical treatment was very primitive by today's standards and even with the advent of the Ambulance Corps the outlook was not bright for the sick and wounded.

Bone tired, hot, dirty, hungry, drenched in our sweat soaked uniforms, nature played us a cruel trick. The heavens opened up and the Army of the Potomac began to resemble a huge pack of drowned rats. Everything within sight was soaked. The roads turned into quagmires. Moving our artillery and supply trains became next to impossible. Although we were a victorious army, we were spent. In spite of this there was one more vital task at hand—pursue Lee and deal a death blow to the to the Army of Northern Virginia.

After the disaster known as "Picket's Charge" on the previous day, Lee knew that his army had been beaten. He understood that his army's ability to supply itself off the land in Pennsylvania had been greatly diminished, his long range artillery ammunition had been expended, so his ability to successfully continue the campaign was over.

The Confederate forces started their withdrawal on the fourth, preceded by the long wagon train containing their supplies and including ambulances with as many wounded as possible. The great bulk of their wounded, almost seven thousand, were left behind where they were treated in the Union field hospitals or by surgeons left behind by the Confederates as they began their withdrawal. Early in the morning of the fourth Lee placed General Imboden, one of Lee's lesser known and lesser qualified cavalry leaders, in charge of the wagon train with orders to leave from Cashtown that evening and head directly south where he would cross the Potomac at Williamsport, Maryland. The train consisted of many hundreds of wagons which stretched in a column fifteen or twenty miles long.

It took a day before all the wagons could be assembled and organized, so it was the next day before it could set out and about 8:00PM before Imboden himself could set out for Williamsport. Remember, heavy rains had started to fall on the fourth and they fell on the Confederate troops as well as our own. Not only were the wagons hampered by the heavy rains and terrible road conditions, they were harassed along the way by Union Cavalry as well as by angry civilians. At Greencastle, Pennsylvania they were attacked by angry civilians who hacked at the wheels of the wagons with axes. In the afternoon of the fifth, Union cavalry attacked them and captured over one hundred wagons, taking over six hundred animals and about six hundred and fifty prisoners. The rebels were forced to abandon wagons as they broke down, Imboden having been ordered to stop for nothing. The wounded that were in the trains suffered terribly. The wagons were the Conestoga type and had no suspensions. Not only were they subjected to the severe jolting along bad roads, but when wagons broke down they were simply left by the side of the road. Their only hope was that some kindly person would find them and give them the help and care they so desperately needed.

During the flight of Lee's army and the pursuit by Meade there were actions, but they were mostly fought by the cavalry units. We were not close to the action. I witnessed none of it and will leave it to the reader to avail himself of the many sources that can give a full account of those actions much better than I.

The battle was over. The Army of the Potomac was in pursuit of the Confederate forces. We left behind a scene of utter devastation. Units who were not front-line troops moved in to the site of the battle and were left with the unenviable and gruesome task of cleaning up the battlefield. Capt. Jacob Kohler was a member of the 36th Regiment of the Pennsylvania Volunteer Militia. A letter which he wrote home to his wife supplies a firsthand description of the scene.

"Gettysburg July 10, 1863

After a hard march we have got to this place at last there has been an awful battle here. About 50,000 killed and wounded our Regiment was on the ground today to gather the muskets off the field. The battleground is about 6 miles long and [illegible] there is hundreds not buried yet. Some have a little ground covered on them you can see their hands feet knees and heads above ground. There were hundreds of horses scattered over the ground. They were artillery horses. We are encamped close to the ground. The smell of the dead is not very pleasant but we got orders just now to draw three days rations. I think we will move tomorrow someplace else. The churches are full of wounded and a great many houses are well [illegible]. I heard today that Ralston is about 2 miles from this place in a hospital and wounded bad. His regiment was in this fight so was the 49th and it is all cut up. Very few got out safe. As I have not much time to write except the short letter I would try to better next time. I am well and will so are all the rest and I like soldiering well and have the best kind of an appetite. I can eat hardtack and bacon as if it was the best they good up for eating. I hope this will find you all well and write soon."

Capt. Kohler wrote several additional letters during the following month. His unit was detailed cleaning up the battlefield and guarding prisoners. His letters have remained in the Kohler family, where they are treasured artifacts of the Civil War. To my knowledge they have never been published.

Digressing from the action if I may, there was an incident that occurred which is worthy to note. If my memory serves me correctly, it was at about this time that there was a peddler circulating among the troops. He had a small press and a large supply of blank metal badges. He would engage soldiers in conversation and explain to them the service he was offering. For a small fee he would produce a set of badges with the name and unit of the soldier, to be pinned to their uniform. Then, in the unhappy event that the soldier was killed or wounded he could be properly identified. Having these badges was not uncommon, since this was before the days of government issued identification.

He did a brisk business. Unfortunately he met a very sudden and violent end. I heard two versions of the story. One was that the false bottom of his canteen came apart, revealing the names of various units and their positions. The other was that the heel of one of his boots came off. It had been hollowed out and had the same information tucked inside. At any rate, a rope was produced, a tree was found and one unhappy rebel spy went to see his maker. I still have my badges to this day.

Back to the action at hand, Lee had managed to get a head start on the flight to his home territory. His forces were to the north of Gettysburg when he started his withdrawal and you might think that would cause him problems, but not so. He started his withdrawal after dark on the fourth and took his troops to the west of the Union army and then south as they headed towards Williamsport and an intended crossing of the Potomac. His route was also shorter than that of Meade. As a result, the Confederate forces arrived at the Potomac considerably before the Army of the Potomac. Unfortunately for the

Confederates the Potomac had been made unpassable because of the heavy rains that continued to fall.

After the battle was over Meade delayed at Gettysburg, unaware that Lee had already withdrawn his forces. When it became apparent that the Confederate forces were no longer at Gettysburg, Meade set his forces in motion. He started south on the east side of the mountains. On the fifth, Sedgwick's entire Corps was sent on a reconnaissance mission and encountered the rear guard of Ewell's Confederate troops. Thinking that this was the main body of Lee's army, Meade halted his troops to prepare for battle. As I understand it, numerous misunderstandings about the position of the rebel forces and conflicting orders allowed the Confederates to get away. It is said that Meade adopted a conservative approach and allowed Lee's forces to forge ahead. This is sometimes the reason given as to why Lee's army managed to reach Williamsport considerably before us.

Meade was severely criticized by everybody from President Lincoln on down for his conduct of operations immediately following the battle at Gettysburg. To those critics it must be said, "You were not there!" Dispatches and battle reports did not tell the whole story or give an entirely accurate picture of what really happened.

Critics say that Meade was too timid and not aggressive enough in taking action. Here are some things that his critics ignored or were unaware of. He had been given command of the Army of the Potomac mere days before Gettysburg and realistically speaking had no time to acclimate himself to his new command. Our forces had endured several days of forced marches in the hot days of early summer just to reach Gettysburg in time to save it from being taken over by the Confederate forces. They were exhausted before the battle even began and were forced into a momentous three day conflict without the least opportunity to rest or gather themselves together. The Confederates, on the other hand, had arrived in the vicinity sooner, had not been on an extended forced march and were more rested at the time of the battle.

Lee's forces had commenced their withdrawal under cover of darkness and had a head start with his entire Confederate force. Remember, Meade was charged with keeping his forces between the rebel army and Washington. Supposing for a moment that a portion of Lee's forces had been involved in a feint, and Meade had taken the bait, Washington could have been left exposed to Lee's army. With this real possibility in mind, Meade did not immediately commit his army to the pursuit of Lee.

Meade acted based on the intelligence at hand and the instructions he was charged with carrying out. As result of this intelligence and Meade's orders, Lee's army escaped. However, if he had been drawn into a ruse by Lee the result could have spelled disaster for both Meade and the nation's capital. Given the exhausted state of our army and the less than perfect intelligence obtained by Meade, I and many of my comrades would characterize his actions as prudence rather than timidity, and believe that his reputation should not have been tarnished.

Chapter 15

Lee Slips the Net

UCH of the action that occurred in the days that followed the battle involved actions by the cavalry of the two armies and there were not any really significant battles. Because of the heavy rains during that week, the fields and roads were not at all suitable for mounted battles. Consequently some of the cavalry skirmishes were fought with the cavalry dismounted. Our regiment was not in a forward position so we did not witness the actions ahead of us. We trudged along the muddy roads without knowing where we were headed. Besides our victory at Gettysburg, about the only thing that buoyed our spirits was the news of Grant's victory at Vicksburg. We learned that Vicksburg fell the same day that the battle at Gettysburg concluded. The fourth of July held special meeting for us that year. The union forces sorely needed victories.

Lee's army had managed to reach the Potomac first, but the river was so high because of the heavy rain that the Confederate forces were unable to cross into Virginia. Consequently Lee's forces found it necessary to construct defenses on the Maryland side of the river as they waited for Meade to approach.

The Union army arrived at the site on the twelfth of July, just as the rebels had completed their defensive works. Lee was spoiling for a fight and was dismayed when he found out that the Union troops were preparing defensive works of their own. He was hoping that the Union army would attack his works and be subjected to a vigorous defense mounted by the Confederates.

Meade contacted General Halleck, the Union Army Commander in Washington, to inform him that he would attack Lee the following day "unless something intervenes to prevent it." However after scouting the situation and conducting a council of war with his generals, He decided to postpone his attack for one day and attack in the morning of the fourteenth. That delay proved to be costly. Lee, growing ever impatient with Meade's hesitation to do battle made a decision to withdraw after dark on the thirteenth. His engineers had managed to construct a pontoon bridge and the Potomac had receded sufficiently for him to effect his escape. When morning rolled around Meade's army was left with empty breastworks to its front and no one to attack. Lee's army had once again slipped the noose.

For the next two and a half months our regiment did lots of marching and not too much fighting. Our Corps had been lucky enough to stay in camp four or five miles south of Gettysburg after the battle, until the eighth, and the only action we saw after Lee's retreat was against some rebel pickets on the fifth of July, along the line they had already abandoned. They were left behind as a ruse trying to fool the Union Army into thinking that Lee had not withdrawn his army. Unfortunately, it worked.

We moved away from that terrible field of battle without ever entering or even seeing the town which gave its name to that fierce battle. After several days of marching we finally reached the Potomac.On the eighteenth of July we crossed over into Virginia at Harper's Ferry. Also we welcomed back our Colonel who had been wounded at Chancellorsville. All were happy to see Colonel Beaver again and to know that he had recovered from his wound.

It is hard to imagine the level of exhaustion that had overtaken us, but Henry Meyer of Company A, who was a gifted writer and whom I have already quoted can give us some idea.

"Although we exulted over a great victory won on Pennsylvania soil, and rejoiced over General Grant's success at Vicksburg, yet our return to the sand and mud of Virginia, and the prospect of again fighting over territory so often fought over before, was quite dispiriting. The long and toilsome marches of the campaign which culminated at Gettysburg, the excessive heat, the mental and physical strain of the battle were exhausting to the boys in the extreme. They were emaciated, weak, and many were unable to carry a musket—myself being one of the latter, until we advanced in line of battle on the rebel works at Williamsport, there I picked up a gun belonging to one our men who went home 'without a pass.' Comrade Thos. E. Rove was one of those emaciated fellows; he possessed hardly sufficient corporeal density to cast a shadow. Someone maliciously remarked that his inherited perversity, strengthened by years of practice, was the only reason he did not lie down and permit himself to be buried. He owed his recovery to an almost exclusive diet of blackberries of which there was an abundance all along our route. For some there was more medicinal virtue in blackberries than in a ton of drugs, and scores of soldiers could testify to the fact."

The remainder of July we marched hither and yon without too much action and without the punishing forced marches that had taken such a physical toll on us. We made excursions into Ashley's gap on the twenty-second and Manassas on the twenty-third. Rumor had it that we would be going to the town of Morrisville and our spirits were raised because it had been so long since we had even seen a town. The rumor was correct and we arrived in the vicinity of Morrisville on the thirty-first. This was a big disappointment for us. Not only had Morrisville been a tiny hamlet, it had previously been visited by our friend Mars, the god of war. All that remained was a group of three chimneys, standing as silent reminders of what had gone before.

During the next several months our corps did much marching but little fighting. If there was a special reconnaissance to be done, more often than not the duty fell upon the Second Corps. We liked to think we were special and that is why we earned the special assignments. During that time we earned the title "The eyes of the Army of the Potomac."

Our regiment in particular was justly proud of our performance as well as our appearance. General Francis Walker wrote in his *History of the Second Corps* about us:

"The appearance and bearing of the troops was brilliant in the extreme but among all the gallant regiments which passed the reviewing officer two excited special admiration—the 148th Pennsylvania, Colonel Beaver, from the old Second, and the 40th New York Colonel Egan from the former Third Corps."

Seeing such glowing comments in print swelled our breasts with pride and proved to us that the strenuous regimen that was instilled in us by our colonel had surely paid off.

Chapter 16

Traipsing About in Virginia

W E stayed in camp near the little ruined hamlet of Morrisburg from the end of July until the middle of September. It was during this time that Capt. Doyle, our company commander, saw the light of day and resigned.

This break was sorely needed and gave our tired troops some time to recuperate from the extreme exertions of the last month and a half. At the beginning of that time we received two months' pay, which amounted to twenty-six dollars. President Lincoln had designated August the sixth as a day of Thanksgiving and we observed it in a grove near our camp with the rest of our brigade. The Chaplin of the 81st Pennsylvania Volunteers officiated. I am not sure of what we were supposed to be thankful for. At least we had our lives, and most of us had our health.

I suppose that was enough, given what we had been through at both Chancellorsville and Gettysburg. It is probably safe to assume that when you hear someone telling glowing stories about their time in the army, they were either not in combat or were having serious flights from reality. There were humorous incidents that happened in and around camp and on the march, but we all came to know that war was a pretty grim business. Sometimes we joked and made light of situations just to hide the unpleasantness of it all.

On August the eighteenth we were ordered to march up to the area around Falmouth for the purpose of securing telegraph poles. Later, at the end of the month we drew forty rounds of ammunition, two days rations and were sent up to the Rappahannock on picket duty. We returned to Morrisville on the fourth of September. All fall it was march here, march there, march back again. We really got to know that part of northern Virginia.

Captain Doyle had resigned on the eighth and we left Morrisville on the twelfth of September, went first to Bealton Station, then to Rappahannock Station, next to Brandy Station and then on to Culpepper. From there it was on to Rapidan Station where we stayed for several days. On September twenty-third we received a welcome visit from the paymaster and the next day our regiment was transferred to the Third Brigade.

On the second of October, our division was assembled and called to order so that we could witness the execution of a deserter. Having already described one such happening, I shall refrain from relating the details of this time honored and barbaric tradition. It is not easy to watch one of our own comrades being executed by the very people with whom he had fought. Those who make the rules think that this harshest of all punishments serves as a stern example to those who might think about taking similar actions.

For me and my fellow comrades, it served only to cast a pall of depression over us. No one among us had any idea why the poor unfortunate creature chose to desert. Maybe he was a coward, maybe not. Perhaps a loved one at home lay deathly ill. Perhaps someone dear to him had died and he felt it his duty to comfort those at home. Maybe he had just been through enough. We will never know. We do know that "Military Justice" is swift and certain—not always just.

October the sixth brought us to camp around Culpepper where most of the Army of the Potomac had gathered. We would have been very happy to set up a more permanent camp here, but our adversary had other plans for us. On the following day the enemy's signal flags were observed by our signal officers on Pony Mountain, and they seemed to indicate that General Lee was making an important movement of his troops. We had chased the Confederates this far south, and for some reason unknown to us, the decision was made to retreat. On the tenth our Corps was formed up in line of battle and we spent the next two days on the march, heading back north. Starting in the early morning hours of the eleventh we moved out, crossing the Rappahannock twice. We moved forward towards Brandy Station, anticipating a battle.

It was on this march that Captain Foster of A Company urged the boys to "Be brave and stand up to our work." Those words spread through the regiment quickly, tinged with not a little amusement and sarcasm. At this stage in our military experience cheerleading was not a requirement. We continued our march northward, crossing the Rappahannock for the third time. Our march had started around midnight and we kept going for eighteen hours, so we did not arrive at Auburn Hills till six o'clock that night, making thirty miles that day. We were dead tired, our legs felt like sticks and our feet were like heavy weights that we were forced to drag along. Some of us learned what it was like to fall asleep while marching, only to be rudely awakened as our tired bodies hit the ground. We had to maintain close contact with our foe lest he make some kind of dash towards Washington or managed to encircle us and attack from the rear.

When we finally bivouacked near Auburn Mills, we did so without fires and were cautioned not to make noise. In this game of cat and mouse it was not good for the enemy to know our position. We knew that we were being pursued but did not know the exact extent or location of the enemy.

Our Second Corps was given the duty of rear guard as the army moved north. We were under the command of General Warren who had taken over for the wounded General Hancock. One of the big problems we faced as the army moved along was the fact that the roads were in such a terrible muddy condition. The wagon trains were continually getting bogged down in the mire.

On the thirteenth we had a skirmish with the Confederates and that accounted for only about fifty casualties on both sides. It happened when some of our infantry came upon a reconnaissance party of rebel cavalry. Little did we know that this was a part of Stuart's vaunted cavalry that had set out to raid our wagon train.

Stuart was forced to withdraw because of our great superiority of troops, but unbeknownst and undetected by us they were trapped between our corps and the Third Corps on their northwest and the wagon train on southeast. Stuart avoided detection by leading his troops into a wooded ravine east of Auburn where he waited for the additional rebel forces that would rescue him. He was hiding a mere 300 yards from our bivouac. During that night he sent out six scouts disguised in Union uniforms through the Federal lines to let Lee know of his predicament. As a result, Ewell was sent to Auburn for the purpose of rescuing Stuart.

On the fourteenth we started our movement north but were delayed by the wagons which were again foundering on the muddy roads. Many of the men took the opportunity to make fires and put on coffee after they had reached the top of the hill. The boys stripped off their wet shoes and socks to dry them out by the fires as they sat waiting for their breakfast to be prepared.

Letting down our guard at this time was definitely not a wise thing to do. Stuart was waiting for Ewell's troops, accompanied by Fitzhugh Lee's cavalry. However, when he saw the relaxed attitude of our troops he decided to take action. With him were seven or eight pieces of horse artillery which he placed on a rise about 800 yards from our line and opened up on us. We were surprised but our commanders soon had the First Pennsylvania Light Artillery in position and dueling with the Confederates. There were movements by the troops of both sides, but the battle ended up mainly in an artillery duel with total casualties of about a hundred. At about 11:00 in the morning and after we had fired about 200 rounds both we and the rebels called off the battle. Both sides had accomplished their objectives. Stuart's cavalry had been saved, and our wagon trains had been extricated from the mud and moved on towards their destination at Catlett's Station. This rather minor engagement went down in the books as the battle of Coffee Hill, named after the boys who decided to make their morning brew at the top of a hill.

Coffee Hill most likely set up a victory for our forces later in the day. The Fifth Corps had preceded us towards Bristoe since we had been occupied with the Confederate forces at Auburn. This put some distance between us. The Confederate Third Corps under A. P. Hill came across our Fifth Corps as they were headed north and commenced harassing their rear guard. Warren spotted the confederates and rapidly deployed our forces behind the railroad embankment at Bristoe Station.

As the rebels launched their attack on the Fifth Corps rear guard, we unleashed a powerful ambush on Hill's corps. This was our second action of the day. We were forced to withdraw when Ewell and his Second Corps were spotted coming up on our left. It was a good day for us. Although we had over 500 casualties, the Confederates suffered considerably more with almost 1,400.

We continued our march north, and on October twenty-first, we moved forward and went into camp about four miles east of Warrenton. While we were camped here, on November second, President Lincoln traveled to Gettysburg. He was to speak at the dedication of the cemetery which had become the resting place for so many of our comrades. It was a mere four months after that terrible battle which had claimed so many lives. He rose to speak after the extensive oration of his predecessor and uttered the words which have become known as one of the greatest speeches ever made. These are the words that Abe Lincoln spoke on that day.

"Four score and seven years ago our fathers brought forth on this continent a new nation conceived in liberty, and dedicated to the proposition that all men are created equal. Now we are engaged in a great civil war; testing whether that nation, or any nation so conceived, and so dedicated, can long endure. We are met on a great battlefield of that war. We have come to dedicate a portion of that field as a final resting place for those who here gave their lives that that nation might live. It is altogether fitting and proper that we should do this. But, in a larger sense, we cannot dedicate—we cannot consecrate—we cannot hallow—this ground. The brave men, living and dead, who struggled here, have consecrated it, far above our poor power to add or detract. The world will little note nor long remember what we say here, but it can never forget what they did here. It is for us, the living, rather, to be dedicated here to the unfinished work which they who fought here have thus far so nobly advanced. It is rather for us to be here dedicated to the great task remaining before us—that from these honored dead we take increased devotion to that cause for which they gave the last full measure of devotion—that we here highly resolve that these dead shall not have died in vain—that this nation, under God, shall have a new birth of freedom—and that government of the people, by the people, and for the people, shall not perish from the earth."

Chapter 17

Winter in Camp

THE next few weeks proved to be a period of inactivity. We sorely needed this time. This gave us an opportunity to rest up and relax, something that we really appreciated. Since the beginning of May we had been constantly on the move or in battle. We were exhausted, both physically and mentally. Life now provided us with numerous diversionary activities. The camps were a bustle with such things as greased pig contests, cockfights, and just about any other activity that could help ease the tension and help us forget for a little while, our deadly mission.

The end of November came all too soon, and on the twenty-sixth of November all the levity ceased and we were again on the move. Our army crossed the Rappahannock River at Germanna Ford, as well as other fords and advanced in the direction of Mine Run. This was not to be an easy time for us. The weather had turned very cold and the roads were in terrible shape.

We finally reached our objective and the various units were placed in position to commence our attack. We were in place and ready to go. The signal guns from the artillery had sounded and we were ready for battle. Then, nothing happened.

General Warren had been ordered to make a flanking operation which would, hopefully, cut off General Lee's lines of communication. Warren made the discovery that the Confederates were much better fortified along his lines than had been previously thought. Meade was initially very upset over the failure of the attack to take place at the appointed time, but after conferring with General Warren, the two generals decided that it was not in the best interest to attack Lee's army at that time. Subsequently the attack was called off at the last moment. The men had been in good spirits, in spite of the fact that the cold rain caused them great discomfort and froze as it hit the ground. We had been ready for battle, but the last-minute cancellation seemed to take the spirit out of us. We had no choice but to recross the river and return to the camps we had left just one week before. This was to become our winter home and we set to work building our shelters. In addition to that, we returned to the diversions of the previous month which included balls and horse races for the officers. This is also a time when there were many draftees added to the Army of the Potomac. General Martin T McMahon wrote an article for the series *Battles and Leaders of the Civil War* in which he described the situation.

"At this time the abuses of the conscription system were made manifest to the men at the front by the character of a large part of the recruits who were sent through that agency. The professional bounty jumper to the kidnapped emigrant and street boy, who were "put through" the enlistment offices in New York and elsewhere, came in large numbers, the professionals with the intention of deserting at the earliest opportunity and repeating the profitable experiment of enlisting for large bounties. Their favorite time for leaving was during their first tour of picket duty, and it was found necessary to store a cordon of cavalry outside our own picket lines. A gallows, and a shooting ground were provided for each Corps, and scarcely a Friday passed during the winter while the Army lay on Hazel River and in the vicinity of Brandy Station that some of these deserters did not suffer the death penalty. During the winter the Army grew again into superb condition, and awaited with high spirits the opening of the spring campaign."

Our camp that winter was the best we ever had, and I believe it might have been the best camp to be found anywhere in the Army. There was enough room for us to be spread out somewhat, and it was thoroughly ditched so that we had good drainage. Although the ground was fairly low and not naturally well-suited for such a camp, the deep ditches which we dug solved that problem so that we had a very desirable and comfortable camp. Our quarters were made of logs. We had a door at one end, a fireplace at the other and bunks along the sides. During that winter we were well provisioned with supplies and provided with new recruits as replacements.

It became the duty of the veteran soldiers to train the new recruits and instruct them in all the duties that were necessary to become a good soldier. Our instruction and the training which we gave to the new recruits quite often could not be found in any training manuals, but the practical experience we had gained gave our new boys much knowledge that would prove useful to them once spring arrived and, with its siren song, would call us again to the fields of battle. We were also kept busy with reviews and inspections during our time in camp

The beginning of March brought a major change to our army. General Grant, who had been victorious at Vicksburg, Mississippi, forced a change at the top of the army. He was named to replace General Halleck who had previously been in charge of all the Union forces. General Halleck had been stationed in Washington DC, but Grant chose to make his headquarters with the Army of the Potomac. This situation caused an awkwardness, because many people seemed to be confused as to who was really in charge of the Army of the Potomac, Meade or Grant. Meade, as leader of the Army of the Potomac, often felt that credit for his leadership was unjustly given to Grant

In spite of this awkwardness, the change in leadership at the top proved to be a huge positive step forward for the Union Army. Before being named to be the head of the Union Army, General Halleck had been in charge on the Western front. He was always dressed in fancy uniforms, was considered by many to be very knowledgeable in military matters, but as we have since learned, he was a prime example of the political general. He never left his office but could easily expound on all matters military, dressed in his resplendent uniform. However, under him the Union Army did not win battles.

It was during the period when Halleck was in charge of the Western Army that Grant began to make a name for himself. Some people believe that his successes on that front were achieved in spite of rather than because of General Halleck. Prior to the war, Grant had suffered many setbacks both in his military and civilian life, which will not be rehashed here. He had resigned from the Army and been involved in many unsuccessful ventures. However, when the war started he reentered the Army, rose through the ranks and became a leading general. His successes in the West enhanced his reputation as a leader. As noted earlier, he was the general who was in charge at Vicksburg when that city fell, coincidentally the same day that the Army of the Potomac finally had a triumph at Gettysburg.

After Halleck had been named general in charge of all the Union armies, he had moved his headquarters to Washington. However, he was still an armchair general, still dressed in magnificent uniforms, still maintained a luxurious office in our nation's capital, and still attempted to run the war from his desk.

Grant on the other hand, was constantly in the field, knew what was happening with his troops and had become the leading Union general. To look at him, however, one would never know. He dressed simply, was not an imposing figure. Many people have said that to look at him one might think he was just another ordinary soldier. On top of that he was plagued by rumors of habitual intemperance, and those who resented him would try to use those rumors against him. There was one person who apparently did not put too much stock in the rumors of Grant's habitual drunkenness. It is said that when Abraham Lincoln was informed about Grant's alleged drinking problem he merely said "If you can find out what kind of whiskey he drinks, send a barrel of it to all of my generals."

It was in March, 1864, when Lincoln replaced Halleck as General of the Army. This would begin a new era for the Union forces and its leader. Gone was the comfortable office in Washington. Gone were the fancy uniforms. Gone was the leadership in abstentia. We finally had a leader in the field; one who knew how to fight and how to lead his army. This marked a change in the war and many people believe that it proved to be the largest single factor which culminated in our ultimate victory.

Henry Meyer from Company A of our regiment gave his assessment of the situation in *The Story of Our Regiment*. I believe he expressed the opinion of most of our men.

"He [Grant] had joined the Army of the Potomac to exercise closer supervision over its operations. Thereafter the long-distance generalship from the city of Washington to the American front was to cease. Think of it, a bespangled and beslippered general sitting in a gorgeously upholstered Hall in Washington, and with the aid of several clerks, pretending, as had hitherto been the custom, to direct the maneuvers of an immense army in the tangle of the brush and forests of Virginia."

As stated by Grant in his personal memoirs, Meade offered to step aside so that Grant could name the commander of his own choice to the Army of the Potomac. Grant related that Meade had made the offer to step aside thinking that he would want Sherman to take over command of the Army of the Potomac. According to his memoirs, Grant assured Meade that he had no such ideas in mind and that Sherman was needed elsewhere. He also stated: "This incident gave me an even more favorable opinion of Meade then did his great victory at Gettysburg the July before." Nevertheless throughout the remainder of the war Meade felt as though General Grant acted like a big brother, constantly looking over his shoulder to see if he was performing properly. He also felt that Grant got all the credit for Union victories, and he was blamed when things went wrong. This is reflected in much of the correspondence that Meade wrote, particularly to his wife, during the course of the war.

During the Civil War the Union forces had adopted a specific symbol for each corps, and the soldiers wore the appropriate corps badge on their hat or on their jacket to help identify the unit to which they belonged. In the Army of the Potomac, the First Corps had a cir-

"Ready, Always Ready"

cle, the Second had a trefoil which was the shape of a club in a deck of cards, the Third was a diamond, the Fourth was a triangle, the Fifth was Maltese cross, the Sixth was a Greek cross, the Eleventh was a crescent, and the Twelfth was a star. Also each badge had a specific color representing each division. Red was for the first division white for the second division blue for the third division and green for the fourth division. This system made it much easier for us to recognize the people of our own unit, as well as the people from other units.

Toward the end of March the Army of the Potomac was reorganized. The First Corps was transferred to the Fifth; two divisions of the Third were incorporated into the Second, but permitted to retain their distinctive flag and badge; the other division of the Third Corps was transferred to the Sixth, but directed to abandon its own flag and badge and assume that of the Greek cross. The corps commanders retained were—of the Second, General Hancock; of the Fifth, General Warren; of the Sixth, General Sedgwick. The First and third Corps thus passed out of existence.

"READY, ALWAYS READY"

Chapter 18

Commencing the Spring of 1864 Campaign

THE winter of 1863 to 1864 passed very quickly. We received many new recruits and replenished our supplies including food and uniforms. General Grant had been named to head the Union forces and the Army of the Potomac had been reorganized. There had been time to train the new recruits, so when the time to move out arrived we were ready and in good spirits. We were well-equipped, well rested, well fed, and ready for action. The same could not be said for our enemy.

One of the Confederate generals, Maj. General E. M. Law, gave a description which compared the Confederate forces with ours.

"Meade's army was thoroughly equipped, and provided with every appliance of modern warfare. On the other hand, the Army of Northern Virginia had gained little in numbers during the winter just passed, and had never been so scantily supplied with food and clothing. The equipment as to arms was well enough for men who know how to use them, commissary and quartermasters supplies were lamentably deficient. A new pair of shoes or an overcoat was a luxury, and full rations would have astonished the stomachs of Lee's rugged Confederates. But they took their privations cheerfully, and complaints were seldom heard. I recall an instance where one hearty fellow whose trousers were literally "worn to a frazzle" and would no longer adhere to his legs even by dint of the most persistent patching. Unable to buy, beg, or borrow another pair, he wore instead a pair of thin cotton drawers. By nursing these carefully he managed to get through the winter. Before the campaign opened in the spring a small lot of clothing was received, and he was the first man of his regiment to be supplied.

I have often heard expressions of surprise that these ragged, barefooted, half-starved men would fight at all. But the very fact that they remained with their colors through such privations and hardships was sufficient to prove that they would be dangerous foes to encounter upon the line of battle. The morale of the Army at this time was excellent, and it moved forward confidently to the grim death-grapple in the wilderness of Spotsylvania with the old enemy, the Army of the Potomac."

Unfortunately General Law's description of the morale and the ability of our enemy to fight proved to be all too true. On May 2 we received an order telling us to demolish our camp. We were not at all sure, but were fairly certain the time to move on had come. On May 4 our Corps began to move in the direction of the Rapidan River and we crossed at Ely's Ford on pontoon bridges. The other two Corps of the Army crossed the river further upstream at Germania Ford. Once again the Army of the Potomac entered into that terrible thicket of underbrush and small trees known as the Wilderness. This would be the third time this stretch of land was fought over.

The land reminded us somewhat of our home in Centre County. Although it was not as hilly, there were many deposits of iron ore in the area. As in our home county, furnaces to produce iron were scattered about. Unlike Centre County, however, there was no ready supply of coal to produce the hot fires necessary for the iron making process. Consequently the forests had been harvested early on in order to provide fuel for the iron furnaces. Up until this time visitors to the area can see the remains of some of these furnaces which were part of the early iron making industry in America.

Since the trees had not been replanted, in time they had been gradually replaced by thick underbrush and younger trees which made maneuvering difficult if not impossible. Also, the vegetation made it much more difficult to use cavalry and artillery. Although the Union forces greatly outnumbered those of the Confederacy, our advantage in numbers was offset by the nature of this land, with its hills, gullies, and rugged underbrush. The "Wilderness" was a good name for this godforsaken country.

The new strategy of the Army of the Potomac was to hound Lee's Confederate forces. It was decided that if Lee's army could be effectively destroyed the Union would triumph without the necessity of capturing the Confederate capital at Richmond. With this strategy in mind it was known that with our superior numbers we would be able to suffer greater casualties, lose more battles, and still win the war. President Lincoln and the generals knew this when we launched our spring campaign. They knew that many of our men who crossed into the Wilderness in the fine spring weather with high spirits would not survive the battles to come. That was a price they knew would be paid to achieve ultimate victory.

Before noon on the fourth the Second Corps had reached the site of our battle at Chancellorsville without having contacted the enemy. As we approached this scene of our very first battle we recognized the landmarks and easily recalled our baptism of fire. The scene had changed very little since we had left, heading up north to the fateful battle at Gettysburg. The scars and wreckage of battle were still scattered over the fields and through the woods. The Chancellor House was in ruins and desolation greeted us as we marched along. The sight of desolation and destruction from past battles was something we had already become accustomed to seeing. Little did we know that our next battle was about to begin.

On the fifth of May our Corps moved out in a south westerly direction on the Carpathian Road in the direction of the Po River. We were on the extreme left of the Union army. As we moved forward toward the battle we met the enemy in midafternoon and our regiment experienced some lively combat with the rebel forces. As each division arrived at the battle scene they were immediately thrust into action by General Hancock. This forced Lee to commit his reserves to the left of our line. We continued our fierce fighting with the rebel forces until nightfall, but neither side gained control.

For our new recruits this was their first experience in combat. Those of us who had joined the regiment at the very beginning did their very best to train them when we were encamped for the winter. Despite all that we could show them and tell them there was no substitute for experience. For example, at one point as we were advancing, we suddenly came upon the enemy and one of our men called out to get down. We old-timers immediately threw ourselves flat down on the ground. One of the new recruits responded by dropping down to his knees and promptly received a bullet in the head. There was no time to mourn because we were now in the middle of a fight. We lost many new men in similar circumstances. Those who survived learned quickly from the mistakes of others, and in doing so dramatically increased their chances of returning home when this war would finally be finished.

Our regiment, as part of the Second Corps, held the extreme left of the Union line. The evening of May 5 left us in close contact with the Confederate forces, along the Orange Plank Road. During the night orders were given for the entire Army of the Potomac to commence a general attack at 5 o'clock in the morning.

On May sixth our Corps along with the Sixth Corps attacked along the Orange Plank Road. Accounts in the published story of our regiment differ greatly. The story of Company A says that we were not greatly involved in the fighting on that date. My recollection and the accounts of many of my fellow comrades tell a completely different story. As I mentioned earlier we were on the extreme left flank of the Union line. During the course of the day someone from the Confederate side found an unfinished railroad bed running south of and parallel to the Orange plank Road. Undetected by us, a Confederate force advanced to our left flank along the unfinished railroad bed and launched a surprise attack which resulted in desperate fighting and many losses. The sixth of May would mark what was possibly the worst defeat of General Hancock's career, and possibly one of the worst days of our regiment. By midafternoon we had run out of ammunition and had to resupply as best we could from the rear.

To all intents and purposes, the Battle of the Wilderness ended in the evening of May 6 with another Union defeat. Making matters worse, the woods caught fire and many of our brave wounded soldiers who fell in the woods perished needlessly. Also on that day, the Confederate General Longstreet was seriously wounded. As he rode towards Plank Road, several Confederate troops mistook his party for Union soldiers and they opened fire, wounding Longstreet in the neck and killing one of his subordinates. This had proven to be a very bad place for Confederate generals. It was but a few miles from here that Stonewall Jackson was shot by his own men during the battle of Chancellorsville. Longstreet was not quite so unlucky. Although out of action for some time, he survived.

Something happened after that loss that changed the nature of the Army of the Potomac. There had been a pattern. We would engage the enemy, fight a battle, lose, and retire from the field to lick our wounds. General Grant and the new strategy changed all that. We didn't go home. In spite of the loss we pressed forward. This meant that we would take advantage of our superiority in numbers and equipment to grind the Confederate forces down. It was a strategy that would cost many men dearly but it was also a strategy that ultimately brought us victory and preserved the Union.

I for one, and many of my comrades, were tired of losing battles and then slinking off like a beaten dog with its tail between his legs. The men of our regiment had been blessed with a superior leader who saw to it that we were the best trained and disciplined soldiers possible. We were proud that in spite of our setback at the Wilderness, we would press forward until the ultimate victory.

Chapter 19

Military Science and the Wilderness Campaign

WHEN people write or talk about wars or battles they often referred to something called "Military Science." Many of our military leaders on both sides of this conflict were graduates of West Point. They had been classmates and worked together until this schism which sought to tear our country apart forced them to become bitter rivals on the battlefield. They had received the same instruction, and all things being equal, battles should have been decided on the basis of which side had the superior resources in men and equipment. This was not the case. Many people feel that the Confederates had the best general, but it is a fact that we had far better equipment and many more men. In spite of this, history shows that our opponents won the greater number of battles in this conflict.

It was felt by many that our advantages in men and materiel ought to give us a great advantage. What those armchair generals did not understand that the ground over which we fought took away many of the advantages that superior numbers and equipment had bestowed upon us. At that time, standard practice among armies was to fight battles as set pieces. That is, each side would assemble their forces facing each other, and whichever army could force the other from the field would win the battle. This type of battle was not possible in the Wilderness campaign because of the very nature of the land over which we fought. There were no open fields or other wide expanses where troops could be assembled into battle lines in the conventional manner. Those who have seen the battle sites will understand that because of the uneven nature of the land and the dense underbrush and scrub, conventional lines of battle were difficult if not impossible to maintain.

There is another factor that no one seems to mention. The rebel troops, by and large, came from places which were rural in nature and the men were probably more accustomed to the nature of the landscape and more accustomed to hunting in the woods. Many of the Union forces, however, with their more urban backgrounds were not as accustomed to the rigors of survival and warfare in this harsh and wild environment. Also, to the rebels, we were aliens invading their homeland and they believed strongly in their cause no matter how misguided they might have been.

It seems to me that we could draw a comparison to the early battles of the American Revolution with the Wilderness campaign. In that earlier conflict the American patriots, whom the British referred to as rebels, were a ragtag bunch of ill organized farmers and tradesmen standing up against the well-trained and powerful army of soldiers who were looked upon as invaders. When the well-trained and superbly equipped British soldiers advanced in their proper formations they suffered embarrassing defeats at the hands of those ill trained, badly equipped citizen soldiers who were fighting for their homeland and for principles which they held to be sacred. Conventional military science went out the window as those early patriots sniped away at the British from behind trees and stone fences. The same could be said to a certain extent during our Wilderness campaign.

The Union forces also had an advantage in artillery but it was nullified by the nature of the land over which we fought. To understand this it is necessary to know a little bit about the artillery that was used and how it was used.

First of all the artillery units were divided into what are called batteries. Each battery usually consisted of six guns. The guns and ammunition were carried on a caisson and a limber. These were large two wheeled carts that were hooked together in the middle and gave the effect of being a four wheeled wagon. Since this combination was flexible it moved over uneven ground much more easily than a wagon. When loaded with a cannon and ammunition they weighed about 4,000 pounds. Each combination caisson and limber was pulled by a six horse team. Every gun had a crew of eight men plus four men to handle the horses and other equipment. That meant for each battery there were 72 men and 36 horses. Life was not only dangerous for the artillerymen, battle exacted a heavy toll on the horses that were responsible for moving the artillery. The life expectancy for an artillery horse was very short. The battlefields were strewn not only with dead and dying men but many horses that were killed in battle or were put out of their misery after suffering horrible wounds.

A person could easily understand that moving such heavy pieces through the woods and underbrush was not an easy chore. Nor was it an easy task to maneuver the pieces into the proper position to fire at the enemy. As a matter of fact, it was often hard to determine where the enemy actually was situated. Consequently our superiority in artillery did not materially affect the outcome of the battle.

When you see cannon on display at some landmark or in front of a County Courthouse, quite often there is an accompanying stack of cannon balls alongside. Although such solid shot was used this is not the kind of ammunition which struck fear into the hearts of the opposing soldiers. There were two types of ammunition whose main function it was to kill the enemy soldiers. One was called a shell. It looks like a cannonball but was hollow and contained explosives. When it exploded in the midst of the enemy soldiers it sprayed pieces of its shell in all directions causing massive destruction and loss of life. The other type was called a canister, and that is what it looked like. The canister had rather thin sides and was packed with metal balls. After the canister was fired the sides disintegrated sending a lethal spray in every direction. If you recall Pickett's charge at the battle of Gettysburg, canister from the Union artillery helped to decimate the Confederate soldiers as they made their fruitless assault on the Union line.

Since time immemorial men have sought to make weapons that were bigger and more efficient than those of the enemy. Groups of people first started fighting with clubs and stones. As time passed spears and knives were used, and eventually the bow and arrow became a weapon that could be used for long-range combat. Finally firearms were invented. With firearms it became possible to do battle over greater distances with more telling effect.

At the beginning of the Civil War the infantrymen were using single shot, muzzle loading rifles as the main weapon. Although they could be very accurate, a good rifleman could only fire two or three shots per minute. With each shot the soldier first had to ram a cartridge down the barrel, then pull back the hammer to cock the rifle, insert an explosive percussion cap into the hammer, sight, and then pull the trigger. During the war there were two advances in fairly quick succession that made it possible for one soldier to fire much more quickly. Both of these were on the Union side.

The first of these was the breech loading rifle. Instead of ramming a cartridge down the barrel with the ramrod, the cartridge was inserted into the barrel just in front of the stock so that the process of loading cartridges was much quicker. The next thing that came along in quick succession was the seven shot breech loading rifle. Seven cartridges could be loaded at one time and then fired in quick succession. This meant that one soldier could fire many more shots in any given time period than a rifleman with the muzzleloader. These weapons were first used during the Wilderness campaign.

There were not enough of these new rifles to supply all of the infantrymen. Only the regiments which proved to be the most effective received them. Our Regiment proved to be one of those highly regarded units so we had the distinct privilege of being issued the new repeating rifles fairly early. We received ours in September of 1864. This was a source of pride for our regiment and it made us even more effective. With these new repeating rifles we could fire up to fourteen rounds per minute. Obviously, this meant that we were six or seven times more lethal than the soldier who was equipped with the old muzzle loading rifles. If all the Union forces had been issued these advanced weapons, we would have won more battles more quickly and the war would have ended much sooner.

Chapter 20

On to Spotsylvania

A FTER the Battle of the Wilderness we were soon on the march. General Warren's Fifth Corps followed by our Corps under General Hancock headed southeast along Brock Road towards Spotsylvania Court House. Sedgwick and the Sixth Corps would head towards Chancellorsville on the Orange Plank Road then turned south, followed by Burnside's Ninth Corps.

On the night of May eight the Confederates were building a series of earthworks more than four miles long starting at the Po River and encompassing the Laurel Hill line. It crossed Brock Road and jutted out into a horseshoe-shape, then extended south past the courthouse intersection. There was a weakness in this line, and that was a bulge in the line that became known as the "Mule Shoe," because of its shape. This part of the Confederates line was an exposed salient and became the site of one of the most horrific battles in which we participated.

Our forces were busy building their own entrenchments. During the morning our beloved General Sedgwick was inspecting his Sixth Corps line and one of the soldiers warned him that it was dangerous to be standing in such an exposed place. He responded "They couldn't hit an elephant at this distance." Immediately he was shot through the head by a Confederate sharpshooter and died instantly. It was a great loss to the Union Army.

Our Regiment played a very prominent part in the battle that was to follow. Many refer to it as bloody Spotsylvania. We had the highest number of casualties of any Regiment that fought there on the twelfth of May. We suffered thirty-three killed, 235 wounded and thirty-three missing.

The night before the battle, we had been well prepared. We were to emulate the attack led by the young Col. Emery Upton whose twelve handpicked regiments rushed across the open field without pausing to fire and reload so that they reached the earthworks before the Confederates could fire more than one or two shots. After they breached the earthworks they would spread out on each side and destroy the enemy. When the Confederate forces realized what happened they immediately counterattacked with units from all sectors of the Mule Shoe. Upton's attack could have succeeded but for the fact that there were no Union troops to follow up. He was reluctantly forced to withdraw

Our attack was designed to function in the same manner. However, it was to be the whole Second Corps. The weather was terrible. There was severe rain and fog. Nevertheless we carried on as planned. We received our marching orders at 10 PM. The order was to make no noise and "break it only with the bayonet." In other words, we were not to fire a shot and were to maintain total silence. We started moving at 11 PM and marched forward for two hours in complete silence.

There was inky darkness, chilling rain, and a heavy mist which made the dense woods even more difficult to negotiate. We were led through the darkness by a sole person with a single lantern. Complete silence was maintained by both officers and men. When we arrived at our position we were totally exhausted we slept on our arms, ready for battle. When time for our early morning assault arrived it was postponed till 4:35 AM because of the dense fog.

When the order finally came we moved forward with Col. Beaver. The 148th was in the front line and broke through the enemy's picket line. We were immediately in the rifle pits of the skirmish line. Up until now no shots had been fired. The veterans had maintained complete silence but a new regiment thinking that taking the picket's rifle pits was a sign of victory, broke into cheers. This set off a chain reaction of yelling and dashing on towards the enemy.

The Confederates immediately opened fire with muskets, grapeshot, and canister; making holes in our advancing ranks. We still proceeded forward, filling the gaps. The pioneers who were in the very front broke up the abatis with their axes and our troops broke through the lanes created by our pioneers. The abatis are heavy tree limbs which have been sharpened on the ends and pointed in the direction of the onrushing troops, designed to impede them or stop them completely.

Desperate hand to hand fighting with swords and bayonets broke out. Horrible scenes of death and destruction were everywhere. There was a constant ebb and flow of battle for almost a full 24 hours. A unit of union troops would charge up the hill only to be met by the opposing rebels. After the battle was over General Grant wrote in his report the following:

"The eighth day of the battle closes, leaving between 3,000 and 4,000 prisoners in our hands for a day's work, including two general officers and over 30 pieces of artillery. The enemy are obstinate, and seem to have found their last ditch. We have lost no organization, not even that of a company, whilst we have destroyed and captured one division (Johnson's) and one brigade (Dole's) and one Regiment entire of the enemy."

General Hancock, the leader of our Second Corps, paid this tribute to his men and described the pursuit after the works had been carried:

"They rolled like an irresistible wave into the enemy's works, carrying away what abatis there was in front of the entrenchments with their hands, and carrying the line at all points in a few minutes, although it was desperately defended. Barlow's and Birney's Divisions entered almost at the same moment, striking the enemy's line at a sharp salient point, immediately in front of the Landrum House; a fierce and bloody fight ensued with bayonets and clubbed muskets; it was short, however, and resulted in the capture of nearly 4,000 prisoners of Johnson's division of Swells Corps, twenty pieces of artillery, with horses, caissons, and material complete, several thousand stand of small arms, and upwards of thirty colors. Among the prisoners were Maj. General Edward Johnson and Brig. General George H Steuart, of the Confederate service. The enemy fled in great confusion and disorder, their loss in killed and wounded being unusually great. The interior of the entrenchments presented a terrible and ghastly spectacle of dead, most of whom were killed by our men with the bayonet when they penetrated the works; so thickly lay the dead at this point, that in many places the bodies were touching and piled upon each other."

If one didn't know better you would think we had just won a glorious battle. This is not really the case. At best it would be declared a draw. We had attacked on the Eastern part of the so-called Mule Shoe and after initial success in the very narrow front, the corps lost all unit cohesion and we were strictly fighting as individuals against the Confederate units. At about 6:30 AM, General Grant sent in reinforcements ordering both Generals Wright and Warren to move forward. Our troops attacked on the western side of the Mule Shoe just south of the point. This portion of the line became known as the "Bloody Angle." Brigade after brigade charged up the hill in attempts to breach the

Confederate line. By eight in the morning heavy rain had begun to fall and both sides contested the earthworks made slippery with both blood and water. The battle went on and on with first one side and then the other gaining the upper hand.

All during this phase of the battle and throughout the afternoon, the Confederate engineers were working hard to create a new defensive line some 500 yards south at the base of the Mule Shoe. All this time there was fierce fighting at the Bloody Angle. It continued day and night. At about 4 AM on May thirteenth the rebel soldiers were notified that the new line had been completed and they withdrew from the original earthworks in an orderly manner.

Other people than me who had an opportunity to view the scene during and after the battle said that it had been so intense that they had never seen anything like it. For example, they had observed that substantial trees had been completely felled by the intense rifle fire at the Bloody Angle. Both sides fought back and forth over the same earthworks for a whole day. When ammunition was exhausted they resorted to hand to hand combat with their bayonets, rifle butts or anything else at hand. Corpses and wounded men were lying everywhere, sometimes in layers. One unnamed person put it this way: "Nothing can describe the confusion, the savage, bloodcurdling yells, the murderous faces, the awful curses, and the grisly horror of the melee." Casualty estimates from the battle at Spotsylvania Court House were approximately 18,000 for the union side and 12,000 for the Confederates.

Chapter 21

Our Colonel Remembers Spotsylvania

OUR beloved Colonel, Colonel Beaver remembered Spotsylvania vividly and he put down his thoughts in *The Story of Our Regiment*. This is what he said:

"Waked about 4:30 AM, somewhat refreshed by a short sleep; gave a few short directions to the men, with the word of cheer, and started on a peerless undertaking. Reached and took the rifles on the skirmish line, with no trouble. Advanced a short distance and then commenced the double quick, with a cheer. It was a glorious sight. The enemy opened with musketry and grape and canister. The column wavered was rallied and pressed on, through the abatis and up over the enemy's works and down into their pits. The scene was one never to be forgotten. Prisoners poured through the column by thousands and colors were captured by the score in the whole mass of troops became thoroughly mixed up. The enemy made a vigorous effort to retrieve their lost ground but was unsuccessful. The Sixth Corps coming up, and we retired to reform our line and were, in turn, ordered to support the right of the Sixth Corps. We were here actively engaged and subjected to the most deadly musketry fire. I was struck on this book [the book he was quoting from] by a spent ball. Our loss today about one hundred and twenty-five."

The Colonel continued with his description of that day's battle, sometimes quoting from his diary. It is unclear whether he was setting down personal recollections from memory or quoting from the diary which he wrote at that time. In any case, I believe it is an accurate depiction of what happened to our regiment and its leader on the twelfth day of May, 1864.

"This was the grand assault on Spotsylvania Courthouse, which was unquestionably the most successful of the war. General George H Steuart, commanding the brigade of Johnson's division, surrendered to me personally. He came toward me with the remark:

"I would like to surrender to an officer of rank."

I replied, "I will be very glad to receive your surrender, sir; whom have I the honor to address?"

He replied, "General Steuart."

He was so different in appearance from what I had imagined General Stuart of cavalry fame, to be and, knowing no other General Stuart, I said in a very surprised tone:

"What! Jeb Steuart?"

"No," he said, George H Steuart, of the infantry."

I then asked him for a sword and he looked about in a surprised way and said:

"Well, sah, you all waked us up so early this mawnin' that I didn't get it on."

I expressed my regret that I could not remain with him and could not see him to the rear. At this juncture a trig little Corporal of the Irish Brigade said, "I'll take care of him, Colonel," and, directing him to see the General safely to the rear, I hurried on.

In coming through the abatis at the salient, I had bent and partially broken the scabbard of my sword. Fortunately the piece was not lost but it was rendered unfit for immediate service. One of our men picked up a beautiful little field saber with a steel scabbard, the exact counterpart of which I had never seen, after we entered the enemy's entrenchments. He gave this to me and I carried it afterwards during the remainder of my service. My oldest saber, however, was repaired subsequently and I have both as valued war relics.

As intimated in my diary, we became so thoroughly mixed up that the regimental organization was entirely lost. Encountering a second line of the enemy's works in this confusion and finding that it was impossible to carry them, we retired and began to form our lines outside the salient, the left of which had been carried by us. It was not long until we were ordered to the right and, to our amazement, we marched over two or three lines of battle of the Sixth Corps lying on the ground which had evidently not been engaged. I have never yet been able to understand why this was done. It was not ours to inquire at the time. We marched to the front, and became warmly engaged and kept up our musketry fire till our ammunition was entirely exhausted. I had the file closers gather ammunition from our dead and wounded from the lines and of the Sixth Corps, which were lying in our rear. Although losing heavily, we accomplished but little in this second stage of the engagement. At one time during the musketry fire, I went close to the line to ascertain whether everything was going well, when I saw Sgt. Kissinger, referred to above, coolly cutting a piece of the shelter tent, including the screw upon his ramrod and deliberately cleaning his rifle. He called to me, "Colonel, don't come up here. This is a warm place; you have no business here; we will take care of this," and he kept on cleaning his rifle and speaking in terms to me and to the men who were immediately about him. Such exhibitions of coolness and courage were by no means unusual. They show the extent to which discipline and training, added to natural gifts, and bring the American soldier.

We eventually retired from this position and through what some protection in the rear, although I have no distinct recollection of this, for on Friday, May thirteenth, I note:

"Remained quietly in our works until evening, when we moved to a position some distance in advance, where we threw up a new line of works adjoining the Ninth Corps on our left. This was just the point at which we entered the enemy's works yesterday morning. Many of our killed and wounded were found here. Sharpshooters were very troublesome."

The satisfaction with which I wrote the first words of the entry on the following day can scarcely be appreciated by those who had not shared the fatigues of the five days immediately preceding. Saturday, May fourteen:

"Remained quiet all day."

The last few lines of Colonel Beaver's recollections can give a good example of just how fatigued we were at that time. They reflect the fact that the Colonel was so fatigued by the events of those few days that his personal recollections did not entirely reflect what he had written down at the time of the battle. I believe this is true of us all. The events were so horrible and our fatigue was so great that the facts are not accurately recorded in our brains.

We spent the next few days reorganizing and reorienting our lines. Corps was moved into a position somewhat in advance of where we had been and we threw up a new line of works adjoining the Ninth Corps on our left. This was not particularly happy movement. That point was exactly where we had entered the enemy's works the day before, and we found many of our wounded and killed comrades here. It was also very difficult because of the heavy rain which made movement over the roads treacherous.

Because of the heavy rain which we had endured for five days, Grant notified Washington that he could not resume offensive operations until we had twenty-four hours of dry weather. When he realized that we had moved to a position that was largely undefended Lee shifted some units from Anderson's First Corps in order to oppose us. If we had moved in spite of our fatigue and the heavy rain before Lee shifted his forces we might have met with some success.

On Monday, the sixteenth of May we had an inspection. This was not a mere formality our leaders needed to know that our arms were in good condition, that we were well supplied with ammunition, to be sure that our shoes and uniforms were in proper condition that our haversacks were filled.

The next day we remained quiet until after dinner and were moved to the left and later to form for an attack on our extreme left, before we were in proper position we marched again, and this time to the extreme right.

On Wednesday, the eighteenth of May we moved before daylight and formed the second line for an assault which would prove disastrous for our troops. Our exhausted men were marched from the extreme right to the extreme left. When we advanced, it was discovered much to our dismay we were caught up in abatis, subjected to artillery fire. It was so intense that the Rebs did not even need to use their muskets to repulse our attack. Neither Burnside nor Wright fared any better,

Thus, Grant made the decision to abandon the battlefield. Grant tried an interesting gambit. He ordered our Corps to march to the railroad between Fredericksburg and Richmond, and then turn south. He thought that perhaps Lee would pursue our Corps, thus giving the Union forces the opportunity to strike the Confederates while they were on the march and before they had an opportunity to entrench.

In the meantime, Lee ordered a reconnaissance in force which encountered fairly inexperienced union troops. They attacked these troops who were then reinforced by the First Maryland and then David Birney's infantry division. This minor battle lasted until about 9 PM till Lee recalled his men. Result of this minor engagement was that we did not begin our movement South until the evening of May twentieth. Our Regiment led the movement of the Second Corps but Lee did not fall into the trap. As the campaign continued Grant tried several more times to engage Lee but to no avail. During this time Grant had a distinct advantage over Lee. The Confederate General was afflicted with the bain of all soldiers on both sides in this great war, and which caused untold misery to Union and Confederate soldiers alike; severe diarrhea. He was very ill and was confined to his bed. It is no small wonder that he was not seen on his well-known horse, Travellor, he was transported in an ambulance and performed as well as possible under such severe circumstances.

Chapter 22

Moving on Towards Cold Harbor

THE Army of the Potomac's campaign which started in the spring of 1864 is often referred to as "The Overland Campaign." This included not only "The Wilderness" and "Spotsylvania Courthouse," but the upcoming "Battle of Cold Harbor" and the "Battle of Petersburg" also referred to as "The Siege of Petersburg" because of its long duration. For those interested in learning more about us during this campaign, our regiment was part of the Second Corps, First Division and the Fourth Brigade. Our Corps was commanded by General Hancock, our division by General Barlow, our brigade by Col. Brooke and our regiment by our beloved Col. Beaver.

Our regiment was in the forefront for the next few days. That was either the privilege or the burden of being under the command of a colonel who had been so exacting and rigorous in the training of our Regiment and preparing it for combat. During the time we were in service many senior officers remarked that we looked more like regular Army troops then volunteers. Let our Colonel tell about the next several days as we approached the battle of "Cold Harbor," as he described it in *The Story of Our Regiment*.

"Friday, May 20:

A good night's sleep, orders to be ready to march at daylight, however, marched at 11:00 PM precisely to the left and turned the right flank of the enemy's position.

Saturday, May 21:

Halted a short time at sunrise, having marched all night and then pushed on; cross the Richmond and Potomac railroad two or three times; cross to the Mat and reached Milford, after passing through Bowling Green, a beautiful little town; deployed the Regiment along the banks of the Mattapony; Ford and pushed across to the waists in water; captured a few prisoners under little camp and Garrison equipage; for two or three miles and were relieved by the Second Division, our Brigade being in reserve.

I find in a letter of May 26, 1864 this account of our crossing of the river.

Friday evening last at about eleven o'clock and commenced a great flank movement which resulted in compelling the enemy to evacuate his strong position at Spotsylvania Courthouse and take a position some twenty-five miles nearer Richmond. Our Corps led to the advance, my Regiment in the lead. We were the first to cross the Mattapony, which we did by fording it, waist deep. We took up a strong position around Milford Station, fortified ourselves and waited for the balance of the Army. On Sunday I was sent with my Regiment on a reconnaissance; we went some 5 miles out, met the enemy's cavalry in front and were fired into by our own cavalry in the rear, but fortunately lost none. The next day the Army came up and we marched here, which is some twenty-two miles from Richmond. The enemy are strong in our front and indications are that we will again turn their position which is I believe now being done by other portions of the Army, whilst we hold them in front."

Later, in this same letter:

"It rains as I write, very steadily, but, thanks to my pack mule, we have a tent with us and are perfectly protected against the weather. We are very well fixed for a campaign. I carry with me in my saddlebags a complete change of underclothing have rubber coat and pantaloons, so I can ride a whole day in the rain without inconvenience; [a luxury not afforded the troops]; have our eatables in a pair of panniers carried on 'Nan' and material for a good bed in any kind of weather. The only thing I need badly is a chair and I intend to have one in as soon as I can send to the train."

Having these passages from our Colonel supplies us with some of the details of our march which the enlisted men might not be able to relate. It is natural that the soldiers would not have access to the details of any given movement. What we knew, is that we marched and marched and marched; often through daylight and darkness, choking dust the driving rain. Nobody asked our opinion or told us where we were going. Such is the plight of the infantry soldier. Colonel Beaver continued his narration.

"These extracts recall vividly to mind the all night march, in which our Regiment led the entire Corps in advance of the Army, and especially the beauty of the scene after sunrise as we reached and passed through Bowling Green. It was a beautiful, fertile valley and, not having been overrun by either Army, everything was fresh and beautiful.

It was in striking contrast with all that we had seen and experienced since crossing the Rappahannock. The reference to my pack mule also recalls that beneficent institution. My stable man, who was a detail from Company I, was a natural born trader. He found this little white mule somewhere before we started and bought her for $20.00. I had a pack saddle manufactured and loaded her, as indicated in the letter quoted above. She was a most intelligent and useful animal. Unfortunately, my factotum, was in the habit of getting a little off the track from the temperance standpoint, when he had the opportunity. On one occasion about this time in the campaign he strayed from the strict line of rectitude and lost the mule. The result was that we went to bed without any bed, and practically supperless except for the bounty of some of the men, who gave us some of their hard tack, upon which we thankfully retired. Sometime during the night I heard the most jubilant mule song and wake up to find one of our boys with Nan, which found the Regiment, without the help of her custodian. She was quite as much rejoiced as we were. She remained with us during the entire campaign and, after my military career had closed, I sold her, if I remember, to Captain William H. Humes of our town, who was assistant quartermaster in the Army.

Scenes referred to in the letter above quoted took place on Sunday, 22 May, as to which I quote in my diary:

"Started on a reconnaissance toward the New Bethel Church; had a very pleasant trip; scared up a few of the enemy's cavalry and were fired into by our own; returned in the evening, without losing a man"

Chapter 23

The Battle of North Anna

OUR Corps was advancing along the North Anna when we reached the Chesterfield Bridge, encountered a small party that had created an earthwork. The third division of our Corps began to take fire from that position. Artillery from the Second Corps fired on the Confederate forces and six o'clock in the evening union infantry charged and overwhelmed the Confederates, who were attempting to defend the bridge. The rebels attempted to burn the bridge as they retreated but our sharpshooters prevented them from doing so.

Our leaders did not know how lightly defended the river was at that point and how easy it would have been to get across, so we missed a golden opportunity by not crossing the North Anna River. General Warren's Corps, on the other hand, had crossed upstream at Jericho Mills and established a beachhead on the other side of the river.

Grant had hoped that Lee would take the bait and attack our Corps as we moved along in advance of the remainder of our army, but he did not oblige. By the evening of May twenty-third Lee had observed the union positions and he formulated a plan for trapping Grant. In conjunction with his chief engineer, he devised a solution that could result in another defeat for the union forces. The Confederates constructed a five mile line in the form of an inverted "V" with the point of the "V" on the River at Ox Ford, the only defensible part of the river.

Lee reasoned that the point of his "V" would divide the union forces and allow him to achieve local superiority along one line of the "V." Interior lines could be used as a force multiplier and moved to whichever side of the "V" they were needed. This would create a large numerical superiority for the Confederates and the only way Grant could reinforce his divided Army would be to have them cross the North Anna River twice. This would allow the Confederate forces much more time to inflict losses on Grant's Army.

Lee's plans seemed to be working. The union forces were falling into Lee's strap. General James Ledlie's brigade had been ordered to attack the Confederate position from the west. Ledlie was not known for his temperate habits and unlike General Grant the rumors about Ledlie were true. On this day he was drunk. In his intoxicated state he decided to attack the Confederate position with his brigade alone. His forces were immediately repulsed. He sent a request back to General Crittenden, his division commander asking for three more regiments as reinforcements. Crittenden instructed the officer to tell Ledlie to refrain from attacking until the full division had crossed the river.

In the meantime Ledlie had become completely drunk. Ignoring several artillery batteries on the earthworks, he ordered a charge. As the troops rushed toward the earthworks rain began to fall, and his various regiments became entangled with each other and confused. The Confederates held their fire until Ledlie's troops were at close range and their fire drove his leading men into ditches for protection. As a heavy thunderstorm broke out, the Mississippi troops came forward and shut down our troops.. In spite of his miserable performance he received praise from his division commander and was promoted to a division command after the battle. His behavior continued and after a humiliating failure at the Battle of the Crater he was relieved of command and never received another assignment. More of this later.

In spite of Lee's plans there were intervening factors that prevented Lee from completely defeating the Union forces. One was Lee's sudden severe bout with diarrhea which prevented him from being on the field and directing the battle. Also, General A. P. Hill had become ill with some unidentified sickness at the Wilderness. He had returned to duty but was still sick and it was impossible for him to perform properly. All of Lee's other main generals were either completely exhausted from the battles of the Wilderness and Spotsylvania, wounded, or too inexperienced for command at that level. The frustrated Lee was said to exclaim "We must strike them a blow—we must never let them pass again—we must strike them a blow."

A heavy rain storm which caused a delay was also a factor. Both sides discontinued their actions because of their fear that the gunpowder would be soaked and unusable. The delay prevented the Confederate forces from following up on the advantage created because of Ledlie's drunken behavior.

At about 6:30 in the evening, Hancock informed General Meade that Lee's forces and position was as strong as what he had faced at

Spotsylvania Courthouse. Grant realized that his army had been dangerously divided. He ordered the troops to stop advancing and to build earthworks of their own facing the enemy. He also ordered his engineers to construct pontoon bridges so that the divided wings of his Army would be able to move quickly to support each other if the situation arose. The next two days brought little action. I believe our leaders understood that we could not sustain a frontal assault nor could we outflank either end of the Confederate line.

On May twenty-sixth, after dark, most of our troops quietly crossed back over the North Anna and our Corps remained to protect the fords on the river while the Army of the Potomac moved to the battle of "Cold Harbor."

Chapter 24

Cold Harbor

THE Army of the Potomac continued to move in a south easterly direction of what is known as Cold Harbor. It is a place that is situated about eight miles east and a little north of Richmond. It is neither cold nor a harbor. Many people believe the name came from an English expression. A wayside inn that did not serve hot meals was referred to as a Cold Harbor. Like Chancellorsville it was not a city or town but merely a crossroads with the building. Nevertheless Cold Harbor became the name for one of the bloodiest battles of the campaign. It came to symbolize the needless slaughter of Union soldiers.

As noted earlier, the strategy of the Union forces had changed. The capture of Richmond was no longer the goal for the Army of the Potomac. It was widely known that the Confederate Army could not replace soldiers lost in battle. The Union realized that they had far greater resources in both men and equipment. On the other hand the Confederates did not have that luxury. It was decided among the Union leadership that the main goal would be to destroy Lee's army. Without adequate resources and men the Confederates would no longer be able to carry on the war.

Facing a stalemate at North Anna, Grant quietly withdrew with his forces in an attempt to swing around Lee's flank, leaving our regiment behind in an attempt to hide the fact that Grant had changed his position. We abandoned our position on the North Anna at 11:30 AM on May twenty-seventh. On the twenty-eighth we commenced our march at 6:30 AM and arrived at the bank of the Pamunkey at 1:00 PM. From there we crossed the river on a pontoon bridge, took up a position short distance from the river, which was about eighteen miles from Richmond, and threw up a strong earthworks.

It was on the twenty-eighth, a Saturday, that the cavalries encountered each other at an intersection known as "Haw's Shop." Most of this engagement was fought by the cavalries dismounted. Neither side considered it a clear victory, but it was one of the bloodiest cavalry battles of the war.

The next day was a Sunday, but it proved to be other than a day of rest. We actually had a whole night to sleep and were having church services when we received an order to march. Our division made a reconnaissance on the Richmond Road and found the enemy entrenched on Totopotomy Creek. This is where we drew up a line at the right and to the rear of the Second Brigade. On Monday we made various changes in the line and joined a portion of the second line to charge across the Totopotomy. However we did not cross the river.

On Tuesday we spent the whole night working on our defensive positions. This is quite a job because we had very few tools. We were learning from the example set by Lee's army that whenever we paused in our movements it was absolutely necessary to dig in and create a proper breast works in order to fend off a possible charge by the enemy. We remained in our positions quietly most of the day but at night we crossed the Totopotomy and were forced to throw up new works.

We spent Wednesday, the first of June at our breastworks until we were ordered to move at night. We marched all through the night in the thick and choking dust. Of course the soldiers were never informed as to where we were marching, we just marched. As it turned out we trekked from the extreme right of our line in a southerly direction all the way down to the left. Our Corps arrived at Cold Harbor early in the morning and formed in the rear of General Wright's Sixth Corps. After stopping for breakfast, our regiment was deployed as skirmishers and we advanced to the South beyond the Sixth Corps, thus becoming the extreme left of our line. During this advance we encountered some of the enemy and drove him a considerable distance.

We had been digging entrenchments or marching almost continuously for several days and the men were dead tired. We learned that the original plan was for our corps to attack the enemy on June second but we were so worn out that the attack was postponed to Friday, June third. One good thing happened on the second. It rained. It washed off some of the dirt and grime of the long march and helped refresh us somewhat.

We were told that there would be a general attack the next day and we knew we would be going up against a heavily entrenched enemy. We knew what we would be going up against because of our experiences at the Wilderness, Spotsylvania Courthouse, and The North Anna. The battle was scheduled to start at 4:30 AM on Friday. Through the night and into the morning hours some of the men could be seen with pencil and paper. Some might think that perhaps we soldiers were writing letters to our loved ones at home. This was not necessarily the case. Upon closer observation you could see that they were pinning the papers to their uniforms. We knew what was going to happen. Those scraps of paper were inscribed with the names, units and hometowns of the men who had written them and pinned them to their uniforms.

They were written by veteran soldiers who knew the very strong possibility that they would not survive the day. They did not fear death as much as they feared the fact that they would become an unknown victim on the battlefield, buried in an unmarked grave, their loved ones forever uninformed of the time and place where their lives were ended. Some appended a simple message "June 3, today I died in battle." Many such messages were found among the carnage.

At 4:30 in the morning we started our attack. It was not well coordinated as we were to find out later. Generals Grant and Meade would have been very happy to blame each other for the disastrous result of the ill planned and ill coordinated battle. Neither general gave specific orders to the corps commanders about how they would coordinate with each other and where they would specifically attack the enemy's lines. Also, it became fairly obvious to those who observed the battle that the senior commanders had not reconnoitered the positions of the Confederate Army.

General Smith who was in command of the Eighteenth Corps commented that he was "aghast at the reception of such an order, which proved conclusively the utter absence of any military plan." It is said that he told his staff that the whole attack was, "simply in order to slaughter my best troops." Unfortunately, Smith's comments contained more than a small grain of truth.

As our troops moved forward they were mowed down by the murderous fire from the Confederates. The field was strewn with the dead and dying. Our Corps under General Hancock managed to break through a portion of the rebel front-line on their extreme right. We managed to drive those defenders from their defensive positions in hand-to-hand fighting. We took several hundred prisoners and captured four guns. The rebels struck back, however , and their artillery began to fire on the entrenchments we had captured, turning them into killing pens for our men. The Confederate reserves counterattacked and drove us off.

Before the battle, the army had received many reinforcements. Unfortunately these were not battle hardened soldiers. The bulk of them were members of Heavy Artillery units who had been garrisoned around Washington for protection of the capital. They were very raw and untrained for their new role as infantrymen. Inexplicably many of these units who looked very good in their nice new uniforms, but were totally inadequate, were thrust into the forefront of the battle. For all too many of them it was their first as well as their last time facing the enemy. Published comments about their ability both as artillerymen and infantrymen were less than sterling. Of course we were not privy to the order of battle or the placement of troops, but in retrospect it seems that the people who were responsible for making those decisions seriously erred in their judgment.

We were stationed on the extreme left so it was impossible to observe what was going on to our right, the union line stretched northward for six miles or so and all that we learned of the battle to our right is what we read in newspaper accounts at the time or what was written and subsequently published in articles and books. Human nature being what it is, those people who were in charge and directed the battles generally wrote accounts that would reflect as favorably as possible on themselves. By all accounts, however, the battle of Cold Harbor was an unmitigated disaster for the Union forces.

At around seven in the morning Grant advised Meade to exploit any successes that had been made. Meade subsequently ordered those of us on the left to make another assault. The three corps commanders were unanimous in their objections. Our Corps under Hancock was really the only unit that had achieved any success whatsoever and our leader advised against another attack. Smith out and out refused, saying that it would be "a wanton waste of time," and Wright's men increased their rifle fire but refused to attack.

By shortly after noon Grant realized that the battle had been lost. He wrote to the commander of the Army of the Potomac, General Meade, "the opinion of the corps commanders not being sanguine of success in case of an assault is ordered, you may direct a suspension of further advances for the present," As a result of that disastrous assault, the Union forces suffered up to 7,000 casualties compared to no more than 1,500 for the Confederates.

General Grant had this to say in his memoirs:

"I have always regretted that last assault at Cold Harbor was ever made. I might say the same thing of the assault of 22 May, 1863, at Vicksburg. At Cold Harbor no advantage whatever was gained to compensate for the heavy loss we sustained. Indeed, the advantages other than those of relative losses, were on the Confederate side. Before that, the Army of Northern Virginia seemed to have acquired a wholesome regard for the courage, endurance, and soldierly qualities generally of the Army of the Potomac. They no longer wanted to fight them "one Confederate to five Yanks." Indeed, they seemed to have given up any idea of gaining any advantage of their antagonist in the open field. They had come to much prefer breastworks in their front to the Army of the Potomac. This charge seemed to revive their hopes temporarily; but it was of a short duration. The effect upon the Army of the Potomac was the reverse. When we reached the James River, however, all effects of the battle of Cold Harbor seemed to have disappeared."

Chapter 25

On to Petersburg and
a Prisoner's Tale

AFTER our defeat at Cold Harbor it was time to try a different approach to bring the Confederacy to its knees. One possibility would be a siege and eventual assault on Richmond, the capital of the Confederacy. The leaders decided to use a different approach, so it was on to Petersburg.

Grant figured that if he could bypass Richmond he could take Petersburg and sever the lines of supply into Richmond. This would mean destroying the railroads that led into Richmond from Petersburg. It would have the effect of isolating Richmond and starving it out.

On the night of June twelfth, the union began advancing along its left flank to the James River, so after crossing to the south bank Grant's forces could isolate Richmond by seizing the important railroad junction of Petersburg. The Union Army proceeded to construct a pontoon bridge over 2,000 feet long which crossed the James River. This action was undertaken from the fourteenth to the eighteenth of June. It was very important for Grant because Petersburg was the junction for five railroads that supplied Richmond. Grant was all too aware that fighting battles against Lee's Army held out little chance for success if he were forced to do battle against Lee's entrenched Army. He would therefore attempt to draw Lee into the open or to cut off all of his supplies, making it impossible for him to defend the capital of Richmond

.During this campaign, as in many of the others, the Union forces had an overwhelming advantage in numbers. Throughout this whole period there were approximately twice as many Union soldiers as Confederates. It had become common knowledge during this time. Our leadership, being aware of the extreme shortage of manpower in the South, knew that the Union could afford to lose many more troops and still ultimately prevail.

Also, being well aware that the Confederates could not replace their troops who were killed, wounded or captured, the Union discontinued the practice of exchanging prisoners. Their philosophy was "We can replace our men taken captive but they cannot." As a result many of our comrades who were taken prisoner either languished until the end of the war or died while in captivity. I was fortunate to never be captured but many of my comrades were, some never to return.

Some of those men who did survive the inhumane treatment they received in captivity have told their stories in *The Story of Our Regiment*. Here is the story as told by one of the men who was captured and lived to tell the tale. It was told by John W Biddle, of Company B. It is appropriate to put his story at this place in my narration because he was one of those captured at Petersburg.

"In my service in the Regiment, I took part in eight different battles. The last one, leading up to my prison life, was in front of Petersburg on 16 June 1864, where we made the charge upon the rebel works. I was assisting Sgt. Ward (I think that was his name), the color bearer, in burying the regimental flag, in order to save it, for we saw that we had got too far ahead and could not retreat for the enemy was coming in on us from two directions. After we had buried the colors, Ward said, "Thank God, John, they won't get the flag, if they do get us."

On they came, with the regulation rebel yell, gathered all about us and said, "Hand over your guns, you damned Yanks," and we had no choice but to comply. We were ordered to fall in ranks and do it damned quick or "we will shoot every one of you." So in we got the best we could and then, the orders were given to march and we started for the rear. We had not gone far, until we were ordered to the double quick. They said the Yanks were coming down on them like hell. A rebel officer came riding up and said, "Move them damn yanks up or they'll be taking them from us."

We were taken back to Petersburg and put in an old tobacco house and then the fun began. They took boxes of tobacco and set them in front of us and said, "If any of you Yanks take any of that tobacco, we'll shoot you." We stayed there that night and then they started us for Andersonville Prison. After they had put us on the train and run us down the railroad, they stopped and said they would give us something to eat but they had not enough for themselves, "so you Yanks can do without." We had nothing to eat for three days. While we were there, they would torment us in various ways, taking meat and cornbread and holding it up in front of us and saying, "Yank, are you hungry?" Then they would sit down and eat and say, "We'll starve you Yanks."

We resumed our trip to Andersonville. They put us on the train and we had not gone far until our troops began to shell the train. One shell struck the end of the car that I was in. We were in hope that we would be recaptured by our men before we reached that hellhole of Andersonville. Our hopes failed us and on we went till we got to that dismal place.

It nearly made us sick. They took us off the train, Marched us to headquarters, there they drew us up in line and asked us if we had any money. We said, "No." Then they said, "you are such liars we will search you," which they did, and took all of our money, pocket knives etc., then marched us to the entrance of the prison, where they took our clothes away from us and opened the gates and turned us in naked and hungry, for we had nothing to eat saying, "there is where you'uns can stay."

It was a heartrending site—the naked prisoners in that place. They were nothing but skin and bones. I felt that I could not live long in that place but I did live in it for eleven months. I weighed one hundred and ninety-eight pounds when I went in and seventy when I came out."

Biddle's story is quite extensive and detailed. In it he gives a graphic account of his experiences and an accurate description of the prison. His account of prison life is representative of many stories related by the survivors. I have included representative portions of his story to let the reader know what the brave men who were captured endured. Biddle continues.

"The prison pen was nothing but a pit of sand and lice. The water we had to drink was out of a brook that ran through the refuse of the prison and the rebels would foul the stream in various ways and say it was good for Yank's health. We were on the verge of starvation, they would throw cornbread on the verge of the deadline and tell us to get it, and would shoot anyone who would attempt to do so, saying they got a ten day furlough home for every Yank they shot.

I saw prisoners who were so weak they could not walk shot when not near the deadline. It was a hard task for me and my comrades treated in that way. We were at their mercy and could not help ourselves. We were poor and weak, infested with vermin. Poor and weak as we were and without shelter or fire, the guard would come in and say they ought to kill all of us. They would kick the prisoners in the ribs and order them to get up, when they were too weak to stand.

They brought our cornbread in a wagon and then would load the wagon with the dead men and haul them out, throw them in a trench, without a box or blanket, throw a little dust over them and leave them for the dogs to dig out and eat up."

Biddle's story concludes as follows:

"Later on we had an ounce of meat and an ounce and a half of cornbread without salt and the water part of the time was green with filth and at other times red with blood, but one morning when I got up, it had rained all night and just a short distance from me there was a stream of nice clear water boiling out of the ground. It looked so good it made me shout with joy it was at the edge of the deadline, so I thought I would crawl over and get a drink, but when I got within a short distance, the rebel guard said" If you touch that water I will put a hole through you; go and drink where you have drunk before; it is good for you hogs."

It is hard for anyone who was not there to believe the truth as to the hardships and cruelty that we suffered in that rebel prison. I have often wondered how anyone survived, as poor and weak as we were. I saw men in the prison who you would see were just living, but the rebels would come in their wagon, take them by the head and feet and throw them in for dead, and if they were not dead by the time they got them, to the trench, they would kill them and throw them in.

How can we ever forgive such cruel and inhuman monsters as Wirz, Wynder and Barrett—the man who would take poorer starved men out of the prison and whip them with the cat-o'nine tails till the flesh dropped from their bones and then tell the men to take the Yank and throw him into a hole.

Thank God! I got out after eleven months. I was taken June sixteenth 1864, and got out May sixteenth, 1865."

This is but one of the prisoner's stories related in *The Story of Our Regiment,* but it serves as a representative picture of the extreme privatizations endured by our comrades who had the bad fortune to be captured.

Chapter 26

The Battle at Petersburg Begins

THE battle of Petersburg began on June ninth. The initial part of the battle did not involve the Army of the Potomac, but the Army of the James under General Butler. Parts of that army crossed the Appomattox River on the night of June eighth, although they didn't make very much progress. Although the Confederate line was lightly defended the Union troops made little headway.

The main assault began on June fifteenth, and after several delays, General Smith commanding the Eighteenth Corps attacked at 7 PM driving the Confederates back. Despite his successes he decided to wait till morning to resume his attack, perhaps not realizing how weak the Confederate line was.

In the meantime our corps under General Hancock arrived. Although he was generally considered to be very aggressive and he outranked Smith, he deferred to Smith's judgment and did not immediately attack. It has been said that he was unsure both of his orders and the disposition of his troops. Also, it has been said by some that if he had not delayed, and attacked the Confederate forces immediately, he could have taken Petersburg and shortened the war. However, this was not the case, and the Battle of Petersburg stretched into the Siege of Petersburg.

By the next morning Beauregard had concentrated his men in a defensive line although it was vastly outnumbered by our forces. Grant had arrived, clarified Hancock's orders, placed Hancock in the temporary command of the Army of the Potomac awaiting Meade's arrival. General Hancock placed Smith's Eighteenth Corps on the right, our own Second Corps in the middle and Burnside's Ninth Corps on the left. Our attack began at about 5:30 PM and all three Corps moved forward together. On this day our Regiment lost many men. Company D alone lost nine men. Also on this day the leader of the 148th, Col. Beaver, was wounded. As could be expected, the enemy fought fiercely, although greatly outnumbered. They would rapidly retreat and erect new breastworks to the rear as our troops broke through their lines. General Meade arrived and a second attack was ordered. General Barlow led his division forward and they captured their objectives. Unfortunately the rebels counterattacked his new position and drove him back taking numerous Union prisoners. It was on this day that Biddle and many other of our comrades were taken prisoner, thus commencing their cruel time of captivity.

This was just the beginning 'of what became known as the Battle of Petersburg. It stretched out until the spring of 1865 and also became known as the Siege of Petersburg. Military historians have divided this period of the war into many actions, some of which are also called battles. Of course, our Regiment was not involved in all of these actions, and I have no personal knowledge of many of them, so this book will deal mostly with those actions or battles during the Siege of Petersburg that our Regiment was directly involved in.

The next day, June seventeenth, contained many uncoordinated attacks on the Confederate line. Some were successful. We captured almost a mile of the rebel fortifications and about 600 prisoners. Various attacks on the Confederate lines of entrenchments were not successful including one by General Ledlie's division. You remember his name because of his drunkenness at Cold Harbor. He gave a repeat performance on this day. Throughout the day the rebels had laid out new defensive positions which they occupied that night and finally dispatched two exhausted divisions from the Overland campaign to help defend Petersburg. Both sides had been reinforced and the Confederates now had just over 20,000 men to defend the city of Petersburg against the 67,000 Union troops under Grant.

I should add that this was the first battle where we had come in contact with colored troops in any number at all. Much has been said and written about them, a great deal of it negative. Many times they were given the task of guarding wagon trains and supplies, but they were rarely sent into battle. It was thought by many including many of the officers that they would not be up to the task. Those of us who observed them in battle and fought beside them would beg to differ. They fought with bravery and skill.

The powers that be, however, did not see fit to allow any of our darker hued brothers to serve as officers. All of the officers of these so-called "colored troops" were led by white officers who were recruited from existing units. At least one officer from our Regiment became an officer in a colored unit and his story contained in *The Story of Our Regiment* is largely positive. Also, comment has been made in that book about the deportment of "colored troops" during what was one of our many defeats. That officer in effect said that unlike their lighter skinned brethren they withdrew in good order and maintained posses-

"Ready, Always Ready"

sion of their weapons. Those of us who had never had contact with these former slaves and sons of slaves learned that when we went into action, the only color that really mattered was the red blood we shed on the battlefield.

As you can imagine, the leader of our Army, General Meade, was extremely upset over the Army's failure to achieve any success the previous day against the fairly light Confederate defenses. He had expected his generals to take more initiative, break through the very lightly defended rebel positions and seize the city of Petersburg. As a result of this he ordered the entire Army of the Potomac to attack. Our corps, the Second, and the Eighteenth Corps were ordered to attack at dawn. We are surprised at the rapid success we were having against the rebel line but we did not realize that Beauregard had moved his troops back the night before, so we were basically attacking a vacant position. When we finally encountered their new defensive line our advance ground to a halt and we suffered many casualties as we tried to hold our line.

By noon our forces had regrouped and prepared another attack. The delay, however, cost us dearly. In the intervening time Beauregard had received reinforcements and Lee had come forward to take command of the defenses. The Ninth and Fifth Corps launched an unsuccessful assault and at 6:30 in the evening, Meade ordered a final assault which failed miserably. As had happened so many times before, the Union Army faced defeat, with over 11,000 casualties as opposed to the Confederate side which had about 4,000.

Our side had almost nothing to show from four days of assaults aside from our very high losses. Rather than withdraw, however, Meade ordered the army to dig in, and thus started the ten-month Siege of Petersburg.

As was alluded to earlier, Petersburg was an important railhead and if the railroads supplying Richmond could be severed, the Confederacy would eventually be forced into submission. Consequently not only would the Siege of Petersburg continue, the destruction of the railroads would begin.

After the initial attempts to capture Petersburg proved to be unsuccessful, the Army's next objective was to destroy the railroads that connected Petersburg with Richmond. There were three of these; the Richmond and Petersburg Railroad, the South Side Railroad, and the Petersburg and Weldon railroad. The latter railroad ran all the way to the vicinity of Wilmington, North Carolina, which was the Confederacy's lone remaining port.

Grant ordered a cavalry raid against both the South side and the Weldon railroads; but also an infantry action against the Weldon railroad by troops that were already in the Petersburg area. The Second Corps as well as the Sixth Corps were chosen for this task by General Meade.

Our Corps commenced movement on June twenty-first toward the railroad and encountered rebel troops as we moved forward. By the next morning the gap had opened up between our Corps and the Sixth Corps. My understanding is that while we moved forward, the Sixth Corps, under General Wright, had encountered a significant Confederate force and began to dig in rather than advance. This caused a gap between our two Corps. As we advanced the gap between us and the entrenched Sixth Corps widened.

The Confederate General Mahone saw an opportunity to exploit this gap. He had been a railroad engineer before the war and had personally surveyed the area. He used a ravine that he was familiar with, to hide his approach. Suddenly in the afternoon, the rebel troops emerged to our rear catching our division by surprise, causing much damage and confusion. We managed to rally around the earthworks that had been constructed on the previous night and stabilized our lines. The following day which was June 23, we moved forward to regain the land given up when our troops had been attacked from the rear by Mahone. However, the Confederates had moved back and abandoned the land they had previously occupied.

This action proved to be an inconclusive. The rebels managed to maintain control over the railroad, but we had managed to destroy a short segment of it. We were able to extend our siege lines, however.

Chapter 27

A Confederate General's View
of Petersburg

THE battle and subsequent siege at Petersburg became one of the pivotal points in the war as it wound down, and a good knowledge of what happened there is important in understanding the conduct of the war as it ground to a conclusion. This is why I have chosen some writings of General Beauregard as he described the battle at Petersburg during the second half of June, 1864. His writings are taken from the *Battles and Leaders of the Civil War*, volume number 30 which was published in 1884. Grant and Beauregard had met two years previously at Shiloh which helped propel Grant to prominence in the Union Army and led to his eventual promotion as General of the Army for all the Union forces. Beauregard's background was different from the great majority of Confederate generals. He was a creole from New Orleans, and not a member of the Virginia aristocratic upper crust as were most of the generals that fought on the rebel side. Many felt that his fiery Gallic temperament contributed to his being not fully accepted by some of his more staid colleagues. However, like many of his contemporaries he was a firm advocate of the Napoleonic tactics in battle. One of the main tenants of this philosophy was "Move directly to the loudest sounds of battle." Many people have expressed the opinion that it is this which allowed the Confederate forces to snatch defeat from the jaws of victory in the earlier battle at Shiloh.

Although many of the details in this excerpt do not relate directly to our regiment they do give the reader some insight into the battle and the workings of the Confederate Army. Also, some of the details which may be of interest to the military historian are omitted from this excerpt because they are not necessary to give a proper description of what happened during those four days in mid-June. Moreover, I believe that generals have a way of describing the battles in a manner that is most favorable to themselves. Beauregard begins.

"The movement of the Army of the Potomac to the south side of the James began on the evening of the twelfth of June, and Smith's Corps (the eighteenth) was at Bermuda Hundred on the early afternoon of the fourteenth. From Point of Rocks it crossed the river that night and was pushed forward without delay against Petersburg. Kautz's Calvary and Hinck's command of colored troops had been added to it.

It was with a view to thwart General Grant in the execution of such a plan that I proposed to the War Department [June ninth] the adoption—should the emergency justify it, and I thought it did—of the bold and, to me, safer plan of concentrating all the forces we could readily dispose of to give battle to Grant, and thus decided once the fate of Richmond and of the cause we were fighting for, while we still possessed comparatively compact, well disciplined, and enthusiastic army in the field....[Beauregard goes on to detail the placement of troops and the extremely light defense of the line he was charged to defend. The following passage is telling.]

Strange to say, General Smith contented himself with breaking into our lines, and attempted nothing further that night. All the more strange was this inaction on his part, since General Hancock with his strong and well-equipped Second Army Corps, had also been hurried to Petersburg, and was actually there, or in the immediate vicinity of the town, on the fifteenth. He had informed General Smith of the arrival of his command and of the readiness of two of his divisions—Birney's and Gibbon's—to give him whatever assistance he might require. Petersburg at that hour was clearly at the mercy of the Federal commander, who had all but captured it, and only failed of final success because he could not realize the fact of the unparalleled disparity between the two contending forces.[Beauregard explains that he was, therefore, very greatly outnumbered and had very little chance of success unless he received substantial reinforcements]

Without awaiting an answer from the authorities at Richmond to my urgent representations, I ordered General Bushrod R. Johnson and to evacuate the lines in front of Bermuda Hundred at the dawn of day on the sixteenth, leaving pickets and skirmishers to cover the movement until daylight, or later if necessary, and to march as rapidly as possible with his entire force to the assistance of Petersburg. The emergency justified this action. I had previously communicated to General Bragg upon this point, and had asked the War Department to elect between the Bermuda Hundred line and Petersburg, as, under the present circumstances, I could no longer hold both. The War Department had given me no answer, clearly intending that I should assume the responsibility of the measure, which I did. Scarcely two hours after Johnson's division had abandoned its position at Bermuda Hundred,

Butler's forces drove off the Confederate pickets left there as already stated, until full possession of the lines.

By the sixteenth of June three Federal Corps—Smith's, Handcock's, and Burnside's—aggregating 66,000 men, confronted our lines.[The editors noted that it was more likely 53,000] Opposed to them, I had, after the arrival of Johnson's division, about 10 AM, an effective of not more than 10,000 men of all arms.

Through a sense of duty I addressed the following telegram, June 16th, 7:45 AM, General Lee: "prisoner captured this A. M. Reports that he belongs to Hancock's Corps (Second), and that it crossed the day before yesterday and last night from Harrison's Landing. Could we not have more reinforcements here?"

No direct answer was received to the above. [Other dispatches received by Beauregard from Lee indicate that Lee was unsure of the union positions the three Corps are actually attacking the Petersburg lines. The Union attack did not begin until after 5:00 PM]

The engagement lasted for three hours, much vigor being displayed by the Federals, while the Confederates confronted them with fortitude, knowing that they were fighting against overwhelming odds, constantly increasing. [He says that Birney's division of Hancock's Corps was on the line. That was our division and we were the only union force to have a notable success on that date.]"

He related that hostilities began early on the seventeenth. At this point in his narrative, General Beauregard quoted from a work that he refers to as "Military Operations of General Beauregard," Vol. II,p.232

"Three times were the Federals driven back, but they as often resumed the offensive and held their ground. About dusk a portion of the Confederate lines was wholly broken and the troops in that quarter were about to be thrown into a panic, which might have ended in irreparable disaster, when happily, as General Beauregard with his staff, was endeavoring to rally and reform his troops, Gracie's brigade, of Johnson's division, consisting of about 1200 men—the return of which to his command General Beauregard had been urgently asking—came up from Chaffin's Bluff at last, the War Department had ordered it to move. It was promptly thrown into the gap on the lines and drove back the Federals, capturing about 2000 prisoners. The conflict raged with great fury until after eleven o'clock at night."

Beauregard had realized that he was grossly outnumbered and that it was necessary for him to take immediate action to avoid a costly defeat. Accompanied by one of his engineers they selected another, much shorter line near Taylor's Creek. It was at a convenient distance to the rear and he caused it to be staked out so that an appropriate time his troops would quietly withdraw and fortify the newly shortened line.

Lee was still not convinced that Beauregard was facing the bulk of Grant's Army and indicated so in a telegram. The telegram read "Telegram of 9 AM received. Until I can get more definite information of Grant's movements, I do not think it prudent to draw more troops to the side of the river." Beauregard sent a return telegram to Lee that stated as follows: " Prisoners just taken represent themselves as belonging to a Second, Ninth and Eighteenth corps. They state that the Fifth and Sixth are behind coming in. Others marched night and day from Gaines's Mill and arrived yesterday evening. The Ninth crossed at Turkey Bend, where they have a pontoon bridge. They say Grant commanded on the field yesterday. All are positive that they passed him on the road seven miles from here."

Here is how General Beauregard described the withdrawal of Confederate troops in the early morning hours of the eighteenth of June:

"The firing lasted on the seventeenth, until a little after 11:00 o'clock PM. Just before that time I had ordered all the campfires to be brightly lighted, with sentinels well thrown forward and as near as possible to the enemy's. Then, at about 12:30 AM, on the eighteenth, began the retrograde movement, which, notwithstanding the exhaustion of our troops and their sore disappointment at receiving no further reinforcements, was safely and silently executed, with uncommonly good order and precision, though the greatest caution had to be used in order to retire unnoticed from so close contact with so strong an adversary.

The digging of trenches was begun by the men as soon as they reached their new position. Axes, as well as spades; bayonets and knives, as well as the axes—in fact, every utensil that could be found—was used. And when all was over, or nearly so, with much anxiety still, but with comparative relief, nevertheless, I hurried off this telegram to General Lee [18th, 12:40 AM] 'All quiet at present. I expect renewal of attack in morning. My troops are becoming much exhausted. Without immediate and strong reinforcements, results may be unfavorable. Prisoners report Grant on the field with his whole army.'

But General Lee, although not wholly convinced even at that hour that the Army of the Potomac was already on the south side of the James, long before the dawn of day, on the eighteenth, and immediately after his conference with Major Cooke, sent me this message: 'Am not yet satisfied as to General Grant's movements; but upon your representations will move at once to Petersburg.' "

"READY, ALWAYS READY"

Beauregard goes on to explain that Lee had taken steps to reinforce the Confederate line and that General Kershaw's division of Lee's army had reached Petersburg on Saturday morning, the eighteenth of June. He went on to state that the grand attack ordered by the Union Army was met with some confusion by the enemy because they had been unaware that Beauregard had withdrawn his forces to new defensive positions. He further stated that all the assaults by Union forces on that day were met and repulsed, and he concluded his comments on the days fighting as follows:

"The truth is, that, despite the overwhelming odds against us, every Federal assault, on the eighteenth, was met with most signal defeat, "attended," says Mr. Swinton, the Federal historian "with another mournful loss of life." This was, in fact, very heavy, and exceeded ours in the proportion of nine to one."

The editor of Beauregard's article made the following comment: "General Humphreys, in his 'Virginia Campaign, 1864 and 1865, 'places the Union losses from the fifteenth to the eighteenth of June at 9,064 killed, wounded, and missing."

Beauregard concluded his article by explaining that Lee's Army arrived and the Confederate forces dug in for the Siege of Petersburg.

Chapter 28

The Crater

AFTER four days hard fighting at Petersburg, both sides had fought to a standstill. The Confederates were firmly entrenched in their newly consolidated lines. Lee's Army had finally arrived at the scene and we were about to engage in a prolonged siege. The Ninth Corps, under General Burnside, however, had gained an advance position and were a mere 130 yards from the enemy's main line.

Among his various regiments was the 48th Pennsylvania Volunteers. The regiment was composed mostly of men who had been coal miners from the Schuylkill coal region. Lt. Col. Henry Pleasants had been a mining engineer prior to the war. He suggested to his division commander that they could possibly run a mine under one of the enemy's forts, blow it up, and gain easy access to the rear of the Confederate line. The proposition was presented to General Burnside who approved it, and work was begun on the twenty-fifth of June, 1864. Our Regiment was not directly involved, but it was an important part of the campaign and the story deserves to be told.

Who better to tell the story than Col. Pleasants himself. He gave testimony before the Committee on the Conduct of the War. This testimony was in *Battles and Leaders of the Civil War*, volume 30. The following is an excerpt of his testimony:

"My regiment was only about four hundred strong. At first I employed but a few men at the time, but the number was increased as the work progressed, until at last I had to use the whole regiment—noncommissioned officers and all. The great difficulty I had was to dispose of the material out of the mine. I found it impossible to get any assistance from anybody; I had to do all the work myself. I had to remove all the earth in old cracker boxes; and that pieces of hickory nailed on the boxes in which we received our crackers, and then ironclad them with hoops of iron taken from old pork and beef barrels ... whenever I made an application I could not get anything, although General Burnside was very favorable to it. The most important thing was to ascertain how far I had to mine, because if I fell short or I went beyond the proper place, the explosion would have no practical effect.

Therefore I wanted an accurate instrument with which to make the necessary triangulation. I had to make them on the farthest front line, where the enemy's sharpshooters could reach me. I could not get the instrument I wanted, although there was one at army headquarters, and General Burnside had to send to Washington and get an old-fashioned theodolite, which was given to me,.. General Burnside told me that General Meade. and Major Duane chief engineer of the Army of the Potomac, said the thing could not be done—that it was all clap-trap and nonsense; that such a length of mine had never been excavated in military operations, and could not be; that I would either get the men smothered, for want of air, or crushed by the falling of the earth; or the enemy would find it out and it would amount to nothing. I could get no boards or lumber supplied to me for my operations. I had to get a pass and send companies of my own regiment, with wagons, outside of our lines to rebel sawmills, and get lumber in that way, after having previously got what lumber I could by tearing down an old bridge. I had no mining picks furnished me, but had to take common Army picks and have them straightened for my mining picks.... The only officers of high rank, so far as I learned, that favored the enterprise were General Burnside the corps commander, and General Potter, the division commander."

The work took a month. It is said that it could have been accomplished in a much shorter time had proper tools been supplied. The length of the gallery was over 500 feet and there were lateral galleries of approximately forty feet at right angles to the main gallery. These lateral galleries were where the explosives were to be placed.

The original plan had been that the so-called colored troops under general Ferraro would lead the assault. There were several reasons for this decision. The other divisions in Burnside's Corps had been performing vigorous duties from the beginning of the campaign and were battle weary. The African-American troops and their white officers believed that they had been slighted merely because of their dusky hue. You must remember that the Union Army was strictly segregated. There were no African-Americans in any white units, except for the servants of high-ranking officers. As a matter of fact, our own leader, Colonel Beaver, had his own colored servant named Ike. Also, all of the officers were white, including those in the "colored" regiments.

These troops had been relegated largely to non-combat duty. Those officers who made the decisions were of the opinion that they were not up to the task, or could not be trusted. I must add that this state of affairs continued to exist well into the twentieth century. It was not until several years after my death in 1938 that the United States finally saw fit to desegregate its armed forces. Many men fought and died on the battlefields of this great conflict to preserve the Union and to free that unfortunate group of people who suffered under the slave-owner's lashes. For all too many, freedom did not bring with it equality.

Ferrero's division trained for weeks, preparing for their opportunity to prove themselves in battle. At the last moment, however, both Grant and Meade decided that these union soldiers of a different color would not be given the opportunity to prove themselves in battle. The result was a disaster.

Let one of the officers who led the colored troops tell his story as it appeared in *Battles and Leaders of the Civil War*, volume 30. The following is an excerpt from the story of General Henry Goddard Thomas.

"East of Petersburg, on high ground, protruding like the ugly horn of a rhinoceros, stood the Confederate earthworks, fortified as a battery, which was undermined and exploded July thirtieth 1864. It did a great deal of goring before we destroyed it. Its position enabled the garrison to throw a somewhat enfilading fire into our lines, under which many fell, a few at a time.

For some time previous to the explosion of the mine it was determined by General Burnside that the colored division should lead to the assault. The general tactical plan had been given to the brigade commanders (General Siegfried and myself), with a rough outline map of the ground, and directions to study the front for ourselves.......

We were all pleased with the compliment of being chosen to lead in the assault. Both officers and men were eager to show the white troops what the colored division could do. We had acquired confidence in our men. They believed us infallible. We had drilled certain movements, to be executed in gaining and occupying the crest. It is an axiom in military art that there are times when the ardor, hopefulness, and enthusiasm of new troops, not rendered doubtful by reverses or chilled by defeat, more than compensate, in a dash for training and experience. General Burnside, for this and other reasons, most strenuously urged his black division for the advance. Against his most urgent remonstrance he was overruled. At about 11 PM, July 29th, a few hours before the action, we were officially informed that the plan had been changed, and our division would not lead.

We were then bivouacking on our arms in rear of our line, just behind the covered way leading to the mine. I returned to that bivouac dejected and with an instinct of disaster for the morrow. As I summoned and told my regimental commanders, their faces expressed the same feeling.

Any striking events or piece of news was usually eagerly discussed by the white troops, and in the ranks military critics were as plenty and perhaps more voluble than among the officers. Not so with the Blacks; important news such as that before us, after the announcement, was usually followed by long silence. They set about in groups, "studying," as they called it. They waited, like the Quakers, for the spirit to move; when the spirit moved, one of their singers would uplift a mighty voice, like a bard of old, in a wild sort of chant. If he did not strike a sympathetic chord in his hearers, and if they did not find in his utterance the exponent of their idea, he would sing it again and again, altering sometimes the words, more often the music. If the changes met with general acceptance, one voice after another would chime in; a rough harmony of three parts would add itself; other groups would join his, and the song would become the song of the command.

The night we learned that we were to lead the charge the news filled them too full for ordinary utterance. The joyous Negro guffaws breaking out about the camp fire ceased. They formed circles in the company streets and were sitting on the ground intently and solemnly "studying." At last a heavy voice began to sing, "We-e looks li-ike me-en a-a marchin on, We looks li-ike men-eeer-war."

Over and over again he sang it, making the slightest changes in the melody. The rest listening to him intently; no sign of approval or disapproval escaped to their lips or appeared on their faces. All at once when his refrain had struck the right response in their hearts, his group took it up, and shortly half thousand voices were appraised extemporizing a half dissident middle part and bass. It was a picturesque scene—these dark men, with their white eyes and teeth and full red lips, crouching over a smoldering campfire, in dusky shadow, with only the feeble rays of the lanterns of the first sergeants and the lights of the candles dimly showing through the tents. The sound was as weird as the scene, when all the voices struck the low E (last note but one), held it, and then rose to A with the *portamento* as sonorous as it was clumsy. Until we fought the battle of the crater they sang this every night to the exclusion of all other songs. After that defeat they sang it no more."

The mine had been dug, it was charged with 8,000 pounds of powder, and in all was set for the operation and on the twenty-ninth of July Generals Potter and Wilcox met together at General Burnside's headquarters to discuss final plans for the attack. Remember that these plans were based upon the assumption that the colored troops would lead the charge and while this conference was in progress they received a message from General Meade that Grant had disapproved the plan and that Burnside must detail one of the white divisions to make the initial assault. This was a mere half a day before the action was to take place and would result in the same tragic loss of life as had happened at Cold Harbor.

Burnside went to his three remaining division commanders and had them draw straws to see which one of them would be the lucky winner to lead the assault. The dubious honor fell on General Ledlie's division. This was probably the worst possible outcome. As you remember it was General Ledlie who had been drunk at earlier battles and whose performance turned out to be no better at the crater. Another fatal flaw to the attack was the fact that Meade ordered the troops to push at once for the crest of Cemetery Hill contrary to the original plans. The plan had been for the attacking troops to fan out to the left and right of the crater for the purpose of driving the enemy from their entrenchments, therefore eliminating the danger of attacks from the flank.

The explosion had been planned for 3:30 AM, but was delayed because of problems with the fuses. It was a terrific explosion, when it finally happened, and when the dust and smoke cleared the men charged forward. When they reached the site of the explosion they were utterly surprised at what they found. There was an enormous crater 30 feet deep, 60 feet wide and 170 feet long, filled with dust, great blocks of clay, guns, broken carriages, timbers and men buried in various ways, some up to their necks.

When the battle weary soldiers had reached the crater they attempted to do what they were ordered. They tried to climb the steep walls of the crater in order to reach their objective at Cemetery Hill but to no avail. The Confederate troops gathered at the rim of the crater and were able to fire directly into the crater killing and wounding many Union soldiers. To make matters worse, the crater was beyond the advanced lines of the Confederates, so that as they recovered from the shock of the explosion those rebel troops were able to fire into the rear of our forces.

General Ledlie had ensconced himself in a bombproof shelter away from the action, and despite receiving information from officers who were in the vanguard of the attack, he refused to do anything except order more men into the fray. As a result the crater became packed with the mass of suffering humanity which was unable to escape from the crater because of the steep walls, the rebel soldiers firing into them, and the Union troops steadily advancing and leaving no means of escape. For the enemy it was like shooting fish in a barrel.

It was into this cauldron of death that our colored troops were finally ordered, too late to effect any type of positive outcome to the battle. They, like the troops who had preceded them, were subjected to the merciless fire of the Confederate soldiers above them. These men who had waited so long to prove themselves in battle and had trained so hard and diligently had now become mere cannon fodder.

Our regiment was not directly involved in this assault, since the Second Corps had been engaged in destroying the railroads and making a feint towards Richmond in order to draw Confederate troops from Petersburg and to disrupt the supplies to Richmond. By the time we arrived back at the site there was not much the Second Corps could do. One of our regiment who had observed the aftermath of this horrible defeat commented about his observations. As told earlier, he said that the colored troops when they were forced to withdraw did so in good order and carried their weapons with them as opposed to many of their white counterparts who had merely dropped their weapons and run. It is no wonder that the song was never heard again.

General Grant wrote, "It was the saddest affair I have witnessed in the war." Our side suffered almost 3,800 casualties. The Confederates by comparison suffered approximately 1,500.

Chapter 29

The Campaign Continues

IMMEDIATELY after the disaster at the crater our Second Corps under Hancock was ordered to advance toward the Confederate capital at Richmond. We crossed the James River on steamships during the night of August 13th, and slowly moved into position for what was to become known as the second battle of Deep Bottom. Remember that this was in the hottest part of the summer and we lost numerous comrades because of heatstroke.

Sometime in the afternoon on August 14th our troops made contact with the Confederates. The Second Corps attacked at the point of Fussil's Mill and were able to drive back two Confederate cavalry regiments but were repulsed by the Confederate general, Anderson. General Birney's Tenth Corps had been ordered to make a night March to join us at the end of the line. This movement was delayed because of the difficult terrain and the plan to attack on August 15th was consequently abandoned for the day.

On the sixteenth we continued our fight against the Confederates and opened the gap but the heavily wooded terrain on which we were fighting prevented the generals from understanding that they had achieved an advantage until it was too late. The confederates rearranged their lines, were able to fill the gap, and drove us back. We stayed in position until the twentieth of August when we withdrew back across the James River.

This was a very bad time for our Corps. The weather was very hot, we had been in combat for an extended time, we were worn out and many men succumbed to heat exhaustion. By the twenty-fourth of August our Corps under General Hancock was ordered to Reams Station in order to destroy as much of the Weldon railroad as possible. The next day was one of the worst days for both the Second Corps and for our Regiment.

Although we had earned the reputation for being one of the outstanding units in the Army of the Potomac, that day was probably our worst experience. We had been in combat for an extended time, our ranks were severely depleted and we had many untrained replacements who were not accustomed to the rigors of the battle. When ordered forward, many men refused to move. To make matters worse, that was the day we lost our colonel while we were in the act of destroying the railroad. He wrote about it in *The Story of Our Regiment*. During the first paragraph he talked about returning to duty after suffering an earlier wound. What follows that paragraph is his recounting of what happened to him at Reams Station. This is what he said.

"The wound which I received was in the left side and was a very painful one and the issue of it quite uncertain for a time. I remained with the Army for a day or two, when I was moved to City Point and sent by slow degrees to my home. Returned to the Army Friday, the 29th of July. I found, however, on reaching there, that I was utterly unable to ride on horseback and after spending two or three days at General Hancock's headquarters, during which the explosion of the mine and what followed it occurred, I was compelled to return home.

I rejoined the Army Wednesday, August 24th. An ambulance met me at City Point, in which I journeyed to the wagon train of the Second Corps and found that our division in company with other portions of the Corps had gone to Reams Station. I followed the next morning in the ambulance and had a very tiresome journey, joining the Corps, or so much of it as was with General Hancock at Reams Station, where they were engaged in tearing up the Weldon Railroad. As I reached the vicinity of Reams Station and was driving in to join the troops, I found our cavalry on both flanks of our infantry engaged with the enemy's cavalry, so that their fire came from both directions across the road on which I was traveling. This indicated that the force engaged in tearing up the railroad was nearly surrounded. I passed that point of danger, however, safely and reported to General Hancock. He seemed very glad to see me and directed me to join my Brigade. He said:

'You are just in time; your Brigade needs you today.'

Being without a horse, I borrowed one from our regimental Quartermaster which I think belonged to Colonel Fairlamb. General Miles, who was commanding the Division that day, was in some other part of the field and I had no opportunity of communicating with him. I rode along the lines for a little distance to find what my connections were and returned to the center of the Brigade, [At this point the Colonel dismounted and proceeded on foot, not wanting to have his borrowed horse shot. He then continues his story] it was quite apparent that the cavalry had disclosed the position of the enemy, and that our infantry skirmishers were engaged. The cavalry started for the rear, their work being done, and as they approached the railroad embankment, I suddenly fell, with my right leg almost at right angles to my body. My first thought was that the cavalry would tramp me to death. I raised myself on the right elbow, finding that I was unable to rise, shook my arm in the air and the leaders of the column of fours rained in their horses and sent the squadron or battalion around me, thus saving me from the danger which I had apprehended. Two of the men who halted dismounted, giving their horses to their comrades, and drag to me from the place I had fallen, until we encountered stretcher bearers who carried me to the field hospital, where a slight examination was made of my wound and I was put into the ambulance which had brought me to the front. My leg was amputated the next morning, the amputation being very skillfully made by Dr. J.W. Wishart, the chief of the operating staff, Surgeon of the 148th Pennsylvania Regiment, my own Surgeon, Dr. Davis, and Dr. George L Potter, surgeon of the 145th Pennsylvania Volunteers, being present. Fearing to be taken to the hospital, I begged to remain with the troops at our field hospital. The men of our drum Corps arranged a stretcher with a canopy made of shelter tents over it, and carried me the entire distance from the point at which my amputation was made to the field hospital, about 7 miles."

Thus ended the military career of our colonel. Because of the immediate and expert medical care he received, he was fortunate to survive, as was the great state of Pennsylvania, since he went on to become our governor.

"Ready, Always Ready"

Chapter 30

The Siege at Petersburg

FOR the Army of the Potomac what became known as the siege of Petersburg continued. Much has been written about this time when the war was grinding to a conclusion. A. T. Hamilton was a surgeon in our Regiment and he kept good records of what happened. His recollection of the action at Ream's Station is helpful in letting people know what happened. It is taken from *The Story of Our Regiment.*

"August 22d moved south along the Weldon Railroad, tore up the rails and ties, burned them. After doing much damage fell back to Ream's Station, with the biggest *little* battle of the War was fought, resulting in a loss of 1,500 prisoners, many lives and defeat.

The railroad cut and embankment served as our line of defense in part as well as being an element of weakness. Some raw recruits lately assigned to our Brigade sought shelter in a deep cut thus breaking the continuity of our line, leaving a gap on top of the bank. The rebels got through and by a punishing fire demoralized the green soldiers and turned the flank of our veterans who were heavily pressed in front. Here the lamented David G. Ralston, First Lieutenant of Company C, was killed—a soldier every inch and a gentleman. Joseph Fox, First Lieutenant, of Company G, stubbornly fought hand-to-hand the attacking party until he received seven bayonet wounds in the face and neck. This brave duty soldier survived the score of battles in which his company participated to meet death in civil life at Bellefonte, on a railroad track. Our Colonel, after convalescing from former severe wounds came back upon this battlefield and, while walking to the front, buckling on his sword, was wounded so badly as to necessitate amputation of the thigh" (as related in the previous chapter).

After a month, on September 25th, we moved into Fort Stedman which was very close to the Confederate lines. October 7th was an important day for our Regiment. We were issued the new Spencer repeating rifle. It was a seven shot muzzle loading rifle and gave us great advantages over those troops we faced. We were one of only three regiments in our entire Corps to be issued these rifles. As told by Dr. Hamilton, they were intended for skirmishers and our Regiment was notoriously good at this kind of action. He stated that the rebels asked our pickets, "What kind of a gun have you Yanks got that loads once and shoots all day."

On October 15th we were in the rear at Fort Stedman. Col. Mulholland had taken over as the commander of our Brigade. On the twenty-fourth of that month we changed position from Fort Stedman to Fort Rice which was three miles to the left, and had a skirmish there. The next day we changed position from Fort Rice to the left of Fort Morton. On October twenty-seventh we were involved in a very important action. It is known as the Battle of Boydton Plank Road. Colonel Mulholland who had become a brigade commander gave an account of this action in *The Story of Our Regiment.*

"The Fourth Brigade of the Division, then commanded by the writer, occupied the line immediately opposite the Crater, where the mine explosion of July 30th had taken place, the left of the Brigade occupying Fort Rice and the right extending toward Fort Stedman. The picket firing was brisk during the day, and rumors of the battle, which was then in progress on the left, were flying, and an anxious spirit was manifest among the men in the works. Towards evening General Miles, wishing to deceive the enemy as to the force then holding the Union line, ordered an attack on the works in front to be made by a small party from each of the two brigades commanded by Colonel McDougall and the writer respectively.

About 5:30 P. M., I received an order from General Miles to take one hundred men and make a demonstration on the enemy's works. Believing it quite possible to capture one of the forts on my front, I selected for the attempt one hundred men from the 148th Pennsylvania Regiment. I took the men from this organization because I knew them to be excellent and reliable, and the big consideration was that they were armed with the Spencer magazine rifle, capable of firing seven shots without reloading....

Addressing the men, I told them of the desperate nature of the duty required, and said that no one need go unless willingly. Everyman was not only willing, but anxious to go. As it was impossible to reach the picket line (from which the attack was to be made) in a body, since the sharpshooters were vigilant, and covered the ground between our main line and the picket, I ordered the party to break ranks and go out individually, taking different routes and creeping through the low brush, be able to assemble at a point indicated without being seen by the enemy. In fifteen minutes every man of the party met me as ordered. We were within fifty yards of the object of attack, and, so far, all had gone well. Forming the party into two sections, I ordered one, under Capt. Brown, to run around the right of the Fort and enter the sally port, while the second section was to charge up the face of the banquette slope and gaining the crest, pour their fire down into the works.

Ten of the men were given axes instead of rifles, and were to run ahead, cut the wires that joined the chevaux-de-frise, and open a section for the storming party to get through. The twilight was gathering by the time that was all in readiness, and the orders were to "make the demonstration at six o'clock." As I was about to give the order to charge I looked back and saw a horseman galloping rapidly towards me. He was coming from the direction of division headquarters, and thinking that he might be bringing some last order, I paused until he came up. It was Capt. Henry D. Price, the Adjutant General. He threw himself from his horse and said:

'Colonel, what's up? I have been at the division headquarters, and heard that you were going to make an attack. I'm going along.'

I did not wish him to go, but he insisted upon it, and knowing his value, I finally consented with much reluctance. He drew his sword, unbuckled the belt, and handed it, together with the scabbard, to Lieut. Tom Lee, one of my aides. He said:

'Tom, if I am killed send these to my mother.'

I gave the order, and the gallant little band, leaping over the slight earthworks of the picket line, ran directly for the enemy's fort, not fifty yards distant. With a few blows the axman cut the fastenings that lashed the chevaux-de-frise, dragged out a section, and the party ran through. The attack was a complete success, Brown entering the fort from the rear, and Price mounting the slope from the front. The defenders for a few moments made a gallant defense, but in vain. In ten minutes from the starting of the charge the fort was carried, and all in it were in our possession. It was getting quite dark when the rush was made, and Captain Price had disappeared from my view. I could not see him after he reached the crest, but I heard his voice as he called to the men to follow him, and then I heard him directing their fire. Suddenly his voice ceased, and I felt sure that he had fallen.

As soon as the fort was won, the prisoners were sent into our lines in an effort made to bring in or destroy the artillery, but little could be accomplished with the latter as the noble band that had done so well were now few in number. There was no possibility of getting reinforcements. None could be spared from the thin line that held the Union works, and after holding the Confederate fort for twenty minutes,

I very reluctantly gave the order to abandon it, and return to our own line, and not a moment too soon, for the enemy had begun concentrating a force to recapture the works and their forts, and from the right and the left of the one captured fort they poured a terrible fire on the little band of Union men then in possession."

It was indeed an honor to see the words written by our Brigade commander who spoke so highly of our Regiment. In his article referred to above, he said the following"

"The 148th was the ideal regiment. In battle, on the march, for picket duty, on the skirmish line, for inspection, for any and every day, the model of the command was "ready," always "ready," and because of this, I now feel after all these years (thirty-six years it is since I looked at the "dress parade" of the 148th Regiment for the last time) that I owe an apology to its officers and men in the fear that perhaps on many an occasion I assigned to them more duty than was their just share. Night or day, no matter when, or for what duty called for, I knew that the 148th was always "ready," cheerfully "ready," and hence, when time was a factor in the enemy pressing, I knew where to look for a prompt response and willing hearts; and so, in offering at this late day to make amends for such seeming imposition on those who are now my veteran friends, I can and do, plead justification in view of the excellent qualities of the "Ready—Always—Ready" and so often called upon, although not always "next for duty."

Chapter 31

Final Stages and on to Appomattox

S HORTLY after the Battle of Boydton plank Road, General Hancock resigned from active command in the field because of the wounds he had received at Gettysburg. He was replaced by General Andrew Humphreys. It was time for the presidential election. The results of the voting in our Regiment showed 127 votes for Lincoln and seventy-two votes for McClellan.

At the beginning of December there was a truce declared in order to bury the dead. At that time Companies A, C, F, G and K were garrisoned at Fort Sampson with the remainder at Fort Gregg. On December 9 we had a reconnaissance to Hatcher's Run and the following day we returned to the line. On Christmas Eve the Regiment was united and garrisoned at Fort Cummings. Five days later we had a midnight march of twelve miles to the west, and thence in winter quarters in front of Petersburg.

On the 5th of February we took part in the action at Hatcher's run. We shifted west to the vicinity of Armstrong's Mill. The purpose of this maneuver was to cover the right flank of Warren's Fifth Corps. During this time our advance was stopped, however the Union forces did manage to extend our siege works in the vicinity. On the seventh we were ordered back to garrison at Fort Cummings.

Spring was finally upon us, and with it the last gasps of a dying Confederacy. Our siege of Petersburg had isolated Richmond, our forces outnumbered the rebels by more than two to one and the Confederacy had exhausted its supplies in both men and material. Lee was desperate. He planned to make a surprise attack on our lines that would have the effect of forcing the Union to contract our lines and disrupt any plan Grant may have had to launch an attack against Petersburg.

In the early morning hours of March 25th the attack began. Grant had let it be known that if the rebel soldiers who wished to come forward and surrender their weapons, they would be granted amnesty. General Lee had the parties of sharpshooters and engineers masquerade as deserting soldiers so they could easily gain a forward position, destroy the obstructions and gain easy access to the Union line. The attack was against Fort Stedman and was initially successful in capturing the fort, opening a gap. Our forces reacted quickly, nearly surrounded the Confederates, launched a counterattack against the Confederates and caused many casualties.

Our regiment was not involved in the initial action but during the course of the day we advanced a mile or so and did become engaged with the enemy. After this defeat, the death of the Confederacy had become a certainty. There would be no further opportunity to break the Union lines and all opportunity to launch any kind of successful operation against the Union forces had vanished.

For all intents and purposes the Confederacy had been defeated but it was necessary to play out the string to the bitter end. On the twenty-ninth we moved up to near Boydton Road and filled in the gap between the union line and the new position that had been taken by Warren's Corps. The next day we were in line in front of the enemy's works. The following day our new Corps commander, General Humphreys, sent two brigades from our division led by General Miles forward and we drove the enemy back for two miles. Of course, our regiment was in the thick of things because we had been issued the seven shot repeating rifles, giving us superior firepower. On the first day of April and we marched to join Sheridan's force and joined him the next day. We were in action near the South Side railroad after we joined Sheridan, and spent the next three days in pursuit of the enemy.

William Henry Stevens was a chaplain in our Regiment, and he passed away shortly before *The Story of Our Regiment* was published. His story is told by his son, Chaplain Emery Stevens. In this story he related much information about the end of the war, including letters written by his father. This one was written on March 31, 1865.

"Yesterday we advanced one mile and found the enemy strongly entrenched, but there was not much fighting done on account of the rain which fell in torrents all day and still it rains beautifully. There is heavy firing on the skirmish line at this time but it rained so hard that I think there will not be much done until it slackens. While eating my supper last evening, a shell exploded in the vicinity of my quarters and a very large piece cut my bridal rein in two, passing under Jim's neck and entering the ground on the spot were my tent had been erected but two hours before. I was eating supper about two rods distant. I think my escape providential, for I took my tent down for no particular reason and had been sitting in the rain at a little fire and had the tent been up I would no doubt have been in it."

A memorandum from April 1st supplied more information.

"Soon after I finished writing yesterday morning a furious battle commenced, which continued with short intervals, until dark, at which time the enemy had been driven a mile. Our Regiment suffered severely as usual. I do not know the number of casualties. Our Adjutant [the above mentioned Capt. Price] was shot dead. The Captain commanding our Regiment was shot through the heel, one Lieutenant was slightly wounded, the color bearer was killed just as he was planting the colors on the enemy's works. All is quiet this morning except a little practice on the skirmish line. It has ceased to rain and the weather is fine but the roads are very bad."

Chaplain Stevens continued his father's story. I would guess that the dialogue set forth was constructed from reminiscences the younger Stevens had heard from his father.

"That night after dark, the Regiment quietly moved forward in line of battle. He assayed to go with them when the officer in command said:

'Chaplain, this is no place for you; you will be needed at the hospital before morning.'

'What is up?'

'I do not know, but I believe the Confederacy will fall tonight.'

He went to his quarters, fell asleep and a little after midnight was awakened by the crash of artillery. It made him so nervous that a comrade at his side noticed it and asked:

'Chaplain, are you cold?'

'No.'

'Are you sick, you tremble on?'

'No, the fight tonight is kind of stirred me up. That is the heaviest cannonading I have heard since Gettysburg.'

The impression that fastened upon him that what the officer had said was true. The discharges began to come in volleys. He knew that one line was falling back, standing and falling back again, but which one? He arose and stood at the door of his quarters until he perceived that the volleys were getting farther away, then lay down. When he awoke in the morning, an orderly dashed past to the hospital. He heard the order given to move. Rushing to him he asked:

'Where is the Second Corps?'

'I do not know, perhaps in Richmond.'

'Have they been captured?'

'No man; don't you know Petersburg has fallen?'

Obtaining leave to join the Regiment, he and Jim were soon on their way, leaving the mess to care for the camp outfit.

He kept with the Regiment to the end. On the march General Sheridan dashed by shouting, "Go in boys, we have just captured 3,000 of them down here and old General Early among them."

April 7th, at Farmville, while talking with Brigade Bugler Joseph H. Law, that battle opened. Law had just spoken of his home, his wife and little boy of four years whom he had not seen since his enlistment, and how anxious he was to see them and said, "Chaplain, Lee is on his last legs. He will surrender in a day or two and then we shall soon get home." He turned and rode into the battle and in a few minutes a solid shot swept his head from his shoulders, the last man to fall in the Regiment."

We were on the march the next day and on the ninth day of April General Lee surrendered to Grant at Appomattox Courthouse. We are told that Lee arrived first and was immaculately dressed in a clean uniform which was befitting a momentous occasion. When Grant appeared, he rode up in a mud spattered uniform wearing a government issued flannel shirt, with his trousers tucked in the muddy boots and only his tarnished shoulder straps betraying his high rank as leader of the Union forces.

It must've been an awkward meeting. It was the first time the two had met face-to-face for many years and he briefly discussed their only previous encounter which had been during the Mexican-American war. Grant then offered the same terms of surrender as he had previously:

"In accordance with the substance of my letter to you of the eighth inst., I propose to receive the surrender of the Army of N. Va. on the following terms, to wit: Rolls of all the officers and men to be made in duplicate. One copy to be given to an officer designated by me, the other to be retained by such officer or officers as you designate. The officers to give their individual paroles not to take up arms against the Government of the United States until properly exchanged, and each company a regimental commander sign a like parole for the men of their commands. The arms, artillery and public property to be parked and stacked, and turned over to the officer appointed by me to receive them. This will not embrace the side arms of the officers, nor their private horses or baggage. This done, each officer and man will be allowed to return to their homes, not to be disturbed by the United States authority so long as they observe their paroles and the laws in force where they may reside."

Chapter 32

The War Concludes

THE surrender of the Army of Northern Virginia did not end the Civil War, but it did ensure that it would come to a successful conclusion for us. The Confederacy could not hold out much longer. General Lee had been its preeminent military leader. On the10th of April we were given marching orders and on the next day marched off to Burkeville where we were encamped two days later.

It was here that we received the news of the cruel assassination of our president, Abraham Lincoln, at the hands of John Wilkes Booth. Not only the Army but the entire nation went into deep mourning for our great leader who so tragically was taken from us before the final victory. While camped here the special Confederate force known as Mosby's Raiders disbanded on the twenty-first day of April. On the twenty-sixth, General Joseph E. Johnston surrendered to Sherman.

On the 2nd of May we were again on the march and moving towards Richmond. Two days later Confederate General Richard Taylor, the son of former president Zachary Taylor, surrendered his troops in Alabama. By May 5th we reached Manchester, which is opposite Richmond, Virginia. On that day the Confederate District of the Gulf surrendered making it the last of the Confederate forces east of the Mississippi River to surrender, although there were still pockets of resistance.

The next day was sweet for us. We crossed the James River on pontoon bridges and marched through Richmond, the capital of the Confederacy, on our way back home. While we were marching north, Jefferson Davis, who had fled Richmond, was captured in Georgia on the 10th of May. He displayed his southern gallantry by attempting to escape capture dressed as an old woman. Unfortunately for him, his riding boots and spurs were visible beneath his long dress.

Other small groups of Confederate soldiers surrendered in the South and West as we marched towards home. By the thirteenth we had reached Four Mile Run near Alexandria, Virginia which is just across the Potomac from Washington DC. This is where we encamped. Ten days later we participated in the grand review of the Army of the Potomac at Washington. A week later our Corps was reviewed at Bailey's Cross Roads before a huge crowd of civilians.

On the first day of June we were mustered out at our camp near Alexandria and on the third we broke camp for the last time and marched into Washington. From there we traveled to Harrisburg by rail. On the seventh the Regiment was disbanded at Camp Curtain, the place where we were originally formed almost three years earlier.

Like many of my comrades it was back home. I returned to Milesburg in Centre County, married, raised a family and lived there until I left this earth on January 5, 1938. Many of the brave men from the 148th Pennsylvania Volunteers were not so lucky. They sleep beneath the ground in places like Chancellorsville, Gettysburg, the Wilderness, Spotsylvania, Cold Harbor, Petersburg, and Farmville. They are all gone now and their memories slowly fade, but the legacy lives on. It lives on in the names like Lucas, Meyer, and Ammerman; names still heard in the towns and villages of Centre County, Pennsylvania—Men who fought bravely to preserve the Union.

148th Pennsylvania Volunteer Infantry Regiment Chronology

T HE 148th Pennsylvania Volunteer Infantry Regiment lost 12 officers and 198 enlisted men killed or mortally wounded and 4 officers and 183 enlisted men to disease during the Civil War. It is honored by two monuments at Gettysburg.

1862

September 8 .... Organized at Camp Curtin, Harrisburg under Colonel James Beaver

September 9-10 .... Moved to Cockeysville, Md. and guard duty on Northern Central Railroad

December 9 .... Assigned to Defenses of Baltimore, 8th Corps, Middle Department.

December 9-18 .... Moved to Falmouth, Va. and attached to 1st Brigade, 1st Division, 2nd Army Corps, Army of the Potomac

1863

April 27-May 6 ....Chancellorsville Campaign

May 1-5 ....Battle of Chancellorsville

June 30 ....Colonel Beaver was on sick leave and under the command of Lt. Colonel Robert McFarlane. In an unusual move, the brigade commander, Colonel Edward Cross, temporarily moved Colonel Henry B. McKeen of the 82nd Pennsylvania to command the regiment during the anticipated battle. Cross wanted the veteran McKeen in charge of the inexperienced 148th, which represented half the strength of his brigade.

June 14-July 24 .... Gettysburg Campaign

June 25 .... Skirmish at Haymarket

July 1-3 .... Battle of Gettysburg. The regiment was commanded by Colonel Henry B. McKeen of the 82nd Pennsylvania until he took over brigade command with the mortal wounding of Colonel Cross. Lieutenant Colonel Robert McFarland then took over the regiment.

From the monument in the Wheatfield at Gettysburg:

"The Regiment engaged the enemy on this position in the afternoon of July 2nd 1863.

"Present at Gettysburg 468 offices and men. Killed and died of wounds, 2 officers, 25 men. Wounded, 5 officers, 88 men. Captured or missing, 5 men. Total 125."

July 5-24 .... Pursuit of Lee

July 23 .... Wapping Heights, Va.

August 31-September 4 .... Expedition to Port Conway

September 1 .... Richardson's Ford

September .... Duty on Orange & Alexandria Railroad and the Rappahannock attached to 3rd Brigade, 1st Division, 2nd Army Corps.

September 13-17 .... Advance from the Rappahannock to the Rapidan

October 9-22 .... Bristoe Campaign

October 12 .... South side of the Rappahannock

October 14 .... Auburn and Bristoe

November 7-8 .... Advance to line of the Rappahannock

November 7 .... Kelly's Ford

November 26-December 2 .... Mine Run Campaign

1864

February 6-7	Demonstration on the Rapidan
February 6-7	Morton's Ford
February – May	Duty near Stevensburg
March	Attached to 4th Brigade, 1st Division, 2nd Army Corps
May 4-June 12	Rapidan Campaign
May 5-7	Battle of the Wilderness
May 8-12	Battle of Spotsylvania Court House
May 9-10	Po River
May 12	Assault on the Salient
May 20	Milford Station
May 22	Reconnaissance by Regiment across North Anna River
May 23-26	North Anna River
May 26-28	On line of the Pamunkey
May 28-31	Totopotomoy
June 1-12	Cold Harbor
June 16-18	First Assault on Petersburg
June 16	Siege of Petersburg
June 21-23	Jerusalem Plank Road
July 27-29	Demonstration on north side of the James at Deep Bottom
July 27-28	Deep Bottom
July 30	Mine Explosion, Petersburg (Reserve)
August 13-20	Demonstration north of the James at Deep Bottom
August 14-18	Strawberry Plains, Deep Bottom
August 25	Ream's Station, Weldon Railroad
October 27	Assault on Davidson's Confederate Battery
October 29	Front of Forts Morton and Sedgwick
December 9-10	Reconnaissance to Hatcher's Run

1865

February 5-7	Dabney's Mills, Hatcher's Run
March 25	Watkins' House
March 28	Appomattox Campaign
March 29	Gravelly Run

March 30-31	Boydton Road or Hatcher's Run
March 31	Crow's House, White Oak Road
April 2	Sutherland Station
April 6	Sailor's Creek
April 7	High Bridge, Farmville
April 9	Appomattox Court House. Surrender of Lee and his army.
May 2-12	March to Washington, D.C.
May 23	Grand Review
June 1	Mustered out near Alexandria

Bibliography

Burton, William L.. *Melting Pot Soldiers*. Fordham University Press, 1998.

Furgeson, Ernest B. *Not War but Murder Cold Harbor 1864* Vintage Books, A Division of Random House, Inc, 2000

Gallagher, Gary W., ed. *Chancellorsville, The Battle and Its Aftermath*. The University of North Carolina Press, 1996.

Herdegen,Lance J. *Those Damed Black Hats! The Iron Brigade in the Gettysburg Campaign,* Savas Beatie, 2010

Hessler, James A.. *Sickles at Gettysburg*. Savas Beatie, 2009.

Johnson, Robert Underwood and Buhl Clarence Clough, editors *Battles and leaders of the Civil War,*. Volumes 26 – 32, the Century Company ,1884

Kamphoefner, Walter D. Helbich, Wolfgang, editors and Vogel, Susan Carter, translator, *Germans and the Civil War,* the University of North Carolina Press, 2006

Keller, Christian B. *Chancellorsville and the Germans*. Fordham University Press, 2007.

Kohler, Jacob, *unpublished letters from Gettysburg, July 1863*

Lossing, Benjamin J *A History Of The Civil War*. The Tompkins Art And Portfolio Company,1922

Muffly, J. W. *The Story of Our Regiment A History of The 148th Pennsylvania Volunteers*. The Kenyon Printing and Manufacturing Company, 1904.

Roberts, Edward F.. *Andersonville Journey, The Civil War's Greatest Tragedy*. Burd Street Press, 2000

Tafel, Gustaf, tr by Tolzmann, Don Heinrich. *The Cincinnati Germans Civil War*. Little Miami Publishing Co., 2010.

Tucker, Philip Thomas, *"God Help the Irish" The history of the Irish Brigade'* WcWhiney Foundation Press, 2007

Valuska, David L and Keller, Christian B. *Damn Dutch, Pennsylvania Germans at Gettysburg*. Stackpole books, 2004

The Author

D AVID Kohler is a retired attorney and a former teacher in the
public schools. He has been a lifelong student of history with
a deep interest in the Second World War, the American Civil
War and the people who fought in them. When not writing, Mr.
Kohler is very busy as a musician; conducting and performing in
community bands, teaching wind instruments and performing as a
bagpiper at numerous events. He is a long time resident of Lam-
bertville, Michigan. This is his second book.